THE STUDENT'S GUIDE TO THE JOB SEARCH

by

Emory L. Cooper

Landon Publications

First printing, 1986

Library of Congress Cataloging in Publication Data

Cooper, Emory L., 1950-
    The student's guide to the job search.
    1. Job hunting—United States. 2. College graduates—Employment—United States. I Title.
HF5382.75.U5C66   1986   650.1'4'024375   86-2991

ISBN 0-937355-00-3

Printed in the United States of America

This book is dedicated to my wife, Dale, and to our children, Brandon, Blake and Bethany, who allowed me the time to write it.

TABLE OF CONTENTS

FROM THE AUTHOR

I've had the idea of writing this book since I first entered the job market after college. I found myself in a position where I had my credentials but knew little about the job search, resumé writing, or the art of interviewing. My lack of knowledge about this important part of my career continued to haunt me for several years, until I realized that my first attempt at a job search had been a dismal failure. I felt that I had selected the wrong company and the wrong career path, but I didn't know how to correct the situation.

Since that time, I have gained knowledge in this area. Because I've worked in the field of personnel, the practical aspects of the job search have become clearer to me. This book is an attempt to share some of my information with you, the student about to search for a job. I hope it helps you achieve a greater degree of success.

In my role as personnel manager and part-time college instructor, I am often asked about the various "how-to" aspects of the job search. Almost every day I receive resumés and telephone calls from individuals seeking employment, and they are obviously in the same position I was some years ago. I hope this book will help them.

This hasn't been an easy book to write, but I have enjoyed writing it. This book has taken a long time to complete, and it would not be complete now without the constant encouragement of my family, friends, and colleagues. It would be cumbersome to list them all here, and it's unnecessary to do so—they know who they are.

If you're a college student about to begin looking for a job, I encourage you to seek employment in areas where you feel that you can grow personally and professionally. You can enhance your success in the job market if your goals and professional standards can be meshed reasonably with those of the company. By doing your homework for the job search, you can greatly improve your chances of career happiness.

Take the selection process seriously but keep it in the proper prospective. Work should and can be fun, and if you select a position and a company in that light, your career will be enjoyable.

Good luck, and best wishes for a successful career.

Emory L. Cooper

CHAPTER ONE

Career Planning And The Job Search

How many times have you been asked, "What do you plan to do after you get out of school?" If you are like many other students, you have heard this question more times than you can remember. Some people can answer with exact details of future schooling or career plans, which they have planned carefully over a period of time. Others—the majority of students and a great number of people currently in the work force—will say only that they plan to get a job. If you're asked how you plan to go about getting this job or what type of position you are seeking, you will probably be unable to give clear details. If this is the case, don't panic. This book will help you.

As a student, you have spent many long hours preparing yourself educationally for that moment when you could pursue your chosen career and take your place in society and the work force as something more than a student. As a student, you selected courses that were needed for the particular diploma or degree you had chosen as your goal. You probably had a curriculum outline as well as a faculty advisor, who helped you set your class schedule each term to ensure that you completed your course of study successfully within a specified period. This type of planning is also necessary for the attaining of your career goals within a stated time, but your career planning is not as simple as your educational planning because no one can give you a clearly defined path that guarantees success.

Before you begin your job search, you must map out what you are looking for now and how it will allow you to achieve your ultimate career goal. This is what career planning is all about. Most people lose sight of their careers because they fail to look at a career as a series of steps which, when logically planned, will lead them to the positions they have always wanted. Instead, they look at their careers in terms of dreams and desires; they give little thought to planning each step and the experience that each one offers in the process of building a career.

Failure to plan careers up to and even beyond the first position is probably the greatest mistake made by first-time job seekers. They generally regard their entry into the work force simply as a natural step beyond their educational preparation. They give little thought to the actual positions sought, the future of the positions, and the meshing of personal needs with those offered by their positions or even by their employers. As a result, these individuals usually become disenchanted with their jobs and are forced to re-enter the job market after a short period of time.

This forced re-entry might well require explanation in their later job searches, regardless of the stated reason for the re-entry. One important rule of the job search is that changing employment has a negative connotation if it is done too frequently. If you spoke to five personnel managers about job changes, at least three of them would probably say that any job change that takes place within three years of accepting a position is questionable. Keep this in mind as you consider your career plans. Changing jobs too frequently could create a negative impression in the eyes of future recruiters. To prevent this from happening, think about what you want to do and work towards that goal.

Career Planning

Career planning involves mapping out the details of what you want to do, how you want to do it, and even where you want to do it. In other words, you must set goals for yourself and your career and plan logical steps necessary to achieve these goals. In addition, you must establish times at which you will review your progress objectively.

You should not try to plan your entire career at one time. This task would probably be so overwhelming that you would panic at the mere thought of forty years of work. Instead, consider your career in less overwhelming and more controllable terms. Reduce your forty-year working career into five-year terms and deal first with the current five years. Set goals that are realistic and achievable during this period. Review your goals and achievements at least once a year just to make sure you are still on target with your plans.

These five-years goals make up your career path in that they represent a logical progression from position to position over a period of time. As a first position, for example, you may accept a job as a trainee in an insurance department, with the goal of becoming an area supervisor of that department in three years and a department manager in five. With this goal, you can plan your career progress and development more effectively for the next five years. During that period you should review your progress toward becoming an area supervisor in the first three years and make adjustments to your career as you see fit.

Let's say, for example, that your career is not progressing as you feel it should. You can either adjust your career goals for the current five years or you can seek a new position that is more in line with your career path. Keep in mind that you must be realistic, both when you plan your career and when you review your progress. Your goals must be achievable or you will be disappointed when your career plans are interrupted.

Personal Planning

The other side of career planning is personal planning. Personal planning deals with your career in terms of financial needs, social expectations, place of employment, and the benefits you require, as well as your overall feeling about yourself in relation to your position. For successful personal planning, take the same five-year approach that you used in your career planning to deal with current and future needs. As in career planning, you must be realistic about your needs and financial situation.

When determining some of your present and future financial needs, you will have to do some projecting. If your personal planning is to be effective, you must be realistic; to think that the cost of housing and utilities will not increase during your five-year planning term is dreaming or wishful thinking. By investigating previous increases you should be able to come up with a reasonable projection for the next five years.

In conducting your personal planning, consider the following questions:

> What standard of living do I wish to maintain?
> What salary do I need to meet my financial obligations?
> Considering my financial goals and the time available, can I maintain my social life?
> What location best suits my needs?
> What benefits offered by the employer are important to me?
> What management style best suits my personality?

A closer look at each of these questions will show you why personal planning is so important to your career success.

What standard of living do I wish to maintain?

It is crucial to consider the standard of living you plan to establish after you enter the work force. Some college students have never had to deal with this question because they have been able to maintain the desired standard of living while attending school; either they received parental support or they were willing to work at part-time positions, usually menial jobs, to supplement what they received from parents or from college loans, scholarships, or grants.

Too often students believe that their first needs after graduation are a new job and a new place to live. After working hard for four years to accomplish their goals, many graduates naturally feel that they deserve these things. No one will disagree about "deserving" but unless you are extremely careful, problems will soon arise. You must ask whether your standard of living is reasonable for the position that you are accepting.

In the beginning, you must know what standard of living you can afford as well as the standard of living you want. Unless your parents or other individuals are willing to help you get started, you must move slowly from the affordable standard of living to the desired standard of living. To put it another way, your beginning point is your affordable standard of living and your desired standard of living is your goal. As in career planning, you must work constantly at achieving your goal. You can accomplish this through planning.

You must map out the progression from the affordable to the desired standard of living. Set your goals to allow purchases for apartment furnishings, new clothes appropriate for your new position, and an automobile for dependable transportation. Consider additional needs over the next five years, such as a home, a new car, or the vacation you want to take. If marriage or family is a consideration in your next five years, you must consider what this will do to both your desired standard of living and your affordable standard of living. Don't try to reach your desired standard of living six months after you start your new job. People will understand your circumstances, so try not to overextend yourself financially. Any attempt to do so will cause problems for you and possibly for your career.

What salary do I need to meet my financial obligations?

To answer this question, you must take a personal view of money management. By making a list of all your expenses, either known or projected, you can get an idea of your financial needs. I suggest that you take two different views: one for your current financial needs and one for your future financial needs. This budgetary analysis might be helpful to you:

Expenses	Present	Future
Housing	_____	_____
Utilities	_____	_____
Telephone	_____	_____
Transportation	_____	_____
Insurance	_____	_____
Entertainment	_____	_____
Food	_____	_____
Clothing	_____	_____
Savings	_____	_____
Other	_____	_____
TOTAL	_____	_____

After you have completed your financial checklist, you will have a better picture of your current and future financial needs. Your monthly financial needs depend on your standard of living, but if the total of these expenditures is more than your net pay for the month, you're heading for financial difficulties. To stay within your budget, you must either reduce your financial needs for the month or seek a position that offers a salary sufficient to meet your needs.

There are a variety of ways to reduce your expenses if necessary. You can ask someone to share your apartment and all the household expenses, which can sharply reduce your financial obligations. You can use public transportation, if it's convenient. If absolutely necessary, you can reduce the amount you plan to spend on entertainment or on monthly savings. As long as the amounts are reasonable, I would recommend this only as a last resort. Don't be too willing to give up your social life just to have an apartment in an exclusive part of the city. Sitting home in a nice apartment does get old.

The cutting of expenses is not the only way to remedy the financial situation. Individuals who are just entering the work force often seek part-time employment for a brief period to help them get established. You can certainly find positions that will pay you extra money and not take a lot of your time and energy. If you decide to do this, let me give you a word of advice: your primary job is your career, for which you have worked hard. Don't let your part-time position interfere in any way with the development of your career and your full-time position. If you're determined to work at a part-time job, try to arrange for very flexible hours, especially during the week. You might want to consider working most of your part-time hours on the weekend, but don't over do it. You need to be prepared for next week's work, and to be alert you must be rested.

Considering my financial goals and the time available, can I maintain my social life?

You must give this question serious thought because leisure time is becoming more and more important in today's workplace. Many companies have adopted a four-day work week or "flextime" to allow the employees more control over their own time and give them more time away from the workplace. Some of the more technical positions, such as data processing, now allow some workers to do their jobs at home by means of computer hookups.

If your leisure time is very important to you, seek out positions that will give you the time to continue your social activities. As you investigate the various positions available in your chosen field, ask about the company's views of their employees' personal lives. Not all companies are concerned about their employees' lives after work, but some attempt to incorporate their employees' social life with the working environment by sponsoring events like bowling, golf tournaments, tennis tournaments, or aerobics classes. They may even provide recreational facilities either at the work place or through corporate memberships at health facilities. This trend is increasing, especially in the larger corporations.

As you evaluate your desired career position, take into account the effect of your position on your social life. You may find that offerings by the company will compensate for your leisure time and even be more convenient than your past social activities. Remember: as you evaluate your time for social activities, don't be so zealous in your career goals that you underestimate or ignore your need for some type of social life, including leisure time.

What location best suits my needs?

It is wise to select your job before you select your apartment or house. If you plan to work in a large metropolitan area, it's best to live as close to your job as possible. Otherwise you may spend time and money on the freeway system. Think of your travel time as money. It's helpful if mass transit is available in the town where you plan to live because it will allow you to live further away from your job and to save on automobile maintenance and gas.

Once you have chosen your position, you must determine how far from work you can live. I suggest that you decide the distance on a town or city map and draw a circle around your place of work to show the distance. To complete your decision, you should look at other areas such as shopping, entertainment, and even where your friends live.

If you are moving into a new area, the local Chamber of Commerce should be able to provide you with valuable information about housing, shopping, transportation, and other areas of concern. Don't be afraid to ask questions about any area you select. It's best to know what you're getting into before you make the move. Remember, each move can be costly and very unsettling.

What benefits offered by the employer are important to me?

As you interview with a variety of companies, you will notice that their benefit packages vary greatly. Many companies take pride in their employee benefits, while others offer only the basic benefits because certain benefits are "expected." You must decide what benefits you feel are important to you at this point in your life. Keep in mind that you must plan your benefit needs just as you plan your career. These needs will change as you progress through your life, and you must project possible future needs. Remember that while you may not need certain benefits now, the opportunity to convert to additional benefits in the future will be an asset to you. When you need them, you will have to reconsider the cost of this changeover. What sounds like an excellent benefit now may be expensive in the long run.

You should also consider the affordability of the benefits. Some companies offer programs through payroll deductions at different times of the year, such as profit sharing, stock purchase, and savings plans. You must consider whether your financial plans will allow you to participate.

To help you analyze your present and future benefit needs, use this list:

Benefit	Present	Future
Medical Insurance	_____	_____
Life Insurance	_____	_____
Disability	_____	_____
Pension	_____	_____
Educational Assistance	_____	_____
Vacation	_____	_____
Stock Purchase	_____	_____
Savings Plan	_____	_____
Leave of Absence	_____	_____
Other: _____	_____	_____
_____	_____	_____

By using this checklist and adding others as you hear of them from companies where you are interviewing, you can determine whether they will benefit you now or in the future. Many benefits are essential because you will use them frequently, but others will be of little advantage to you at certain times in your life. Above all, plan your benefit package just as you do your career.

What management style best suits my personality?

The management style of a company should be a part of your personal planning because the atmosphere in the workplace must be compatible with your personality. The style of management practiced by each company determines the office atmosphere, to a large degree. Considering three basic management styles listed below, try to determine which one is practiced by the companies you are interviewing and which style is most comfortable for you. These are the three basic styles, with a brief explanation of each:

> *Autocratic*: In this style the boss controls what happens in the workplace. He or she dictates policies and procedures, and does not seek or accept suggestions about how things should be done.

> *Democratic*: In this style the employees have the opportunity to provide feedback in terms of suggestions and requests, which gives them some influence on the day-to-day operation of the office.

> *Participative*: If the employee exercises a strong sense of responsibility, this style provides the opportunity to demonstrate the ability to do the job. The employee simply keeps the boss informed.

On the basis of these brief descriptions of the different management styles, try to match the style you prefer to the company that has a position available. Use the types of management style to evaluate the personalities and office atmosphere.

Analyzing management styles in a company will not be easy, but if you ask questions about the company's approach to employee relations and career development, you will have a hint of what is present in that company's atmosphere. Let me add a word of caution: not every person in a company operates under the same philosophy, even though it is the company's philosophy. It is difficult to control each manager's style so don't think that you're home free once you've found a company with the style you prefer. When you interview with the person you will be reporting to, try to determine his or her style. If you see that the manager's philosophy agrees with the company's, and if you don't care for the company's style, I'd suggest that you seek employment elsewhere.

To summarize, your career plans and your personal plans must complement each other to ensure maximum success. A personal need for a $30,000 annual salary will create a personal conflict if your position as an insurance trainee pays only $20,000. Likewise, if you feel that a participative management style is essential for your personal and professional success, a position with a company that practices autocratic leadership will prove very unsatisfactory for you. By doing a thorough job of deciding what type of position you are looking for and how you can progress to the next step in your career, you will greatly improve your chances of success.

This analysis is a continuing process, and you should monitor it at least once a year. The best time is at the start of each year, rather than when you get a raise or a promotion. Don't feel that because you are achieving apparent success in your first position (or any position, for that matter), future career and personal planning is unnecessary. If you are succeeding at a faster pace than the goals you set earlier, you must revise your career goals.

The Job Search

Now that you have completed your first review of your career and personal plans, it is time to land that first job, which will set you on your path to accomplishing your goals. You are ready to begin the job search.

The job search involves more than submitting applications for employment with various companies. It requires effort on your part. You must investigate the job market to determine what positions are available in your area of interest as well as the philosophy, the financial position, the projected growth, the dedication to employee development, and your chances of advancement in the companies that offer these positions. All these things are important and deserve serious consideration before you accept offers of employment from any company.

For some time the employment arena was regarded as the exclusive domain of the employer. This attitude was fostered by the lack of mobility in the work force and the willingness of the work force to accept the employer's practices without question. It was the employer who set the guidelines, the salaries, the working conditions, and the career paths of employees with little or no regard for or input from the employees.

This has changed, however, and employment continues to advance from a one-way management-controlled arena to a two-way team effort, where employer and employee work closely for mutual success. A closer look at this transition will give you better insight into the job search process.

Before the technological advancements in our society, the workplace was considered as a location that was reasonably convenient to where one lived. In the past, people lived and worked in a much smaller area. With the advancement of technology, however, the smaller neighborhood has been transformed by the increased mobility of our society, aided by mass transportation. Mass transit systems, combined with the willingness of employees to spend a greater amount of their time traveling to and from work, has greatly expanded the job market for everyone.

In addition, the increased technological development of our society has created a need for specialization in a large number of career fields. The field of personnel, for example, has changed from a single field to a collection of specialized areas such as benefits, compensation, recruiting, and training and development. While this specialization has increased the applicant's ability to channel his or her interest into a more agreeable position, it has also required the applicant to present credentials that show more specialized preparation.

You may be asking, "What does this mean to me in the job market?" The answer depends on different controlling variables for each individual. In order to get the job you want, you will have to prepare yourself not only for the job but for the job search. Take it seriously.

CHAPTER TWO

How To Get Started

Before you begin the actual job search, you must understand several things. You have probably been told throughout your life that in order to get a good job two things are necessary: 1) you must have something to offer the employer; and 2) you must sell yourself as the best qualified person for the job you are seeking. This statement is probably even more true today than in the past. Our advanced technology has had two different results. First, employers are now seeking individuals who have excellent credentials and can offer the employer the skills that the employer needs. Second, in this open market for jobs, applicants are willing to travel outside their usual surroundings to acquire the position they want, and the employers are willing to pay them well. These two characteristics have drawn both the employer and the applicant deeply into the job market. As you enter the job market, you will see that it is an open market; both the employer and the applicant must be fully prepared for it. Those companies and applicants that are not prepared will surely be left behind.

In order to hold your own, you must be prepared to market yourself, your skills, and your ability. This should not be difficult because you have an advantage: you have all the material you need. You merely need to decide what information you want to use in your marketing efforts and how to use that information to your advantage.

The major tool of your job search is the resumé. The resumé is you, the applicant, on paper, giving the best possible picture of your progression to the present time. Your personal information, your education, and your work experience will make up a composite picture of you.

Many people have chosen to have a professional resumé service do all the work for them. I must admit that this method is less time-consuming than writing one's own resumé, but I feel that the applicant is short-changed in the long run. I don't advise hiring someone to write your resumé for you. At a resumé service, a representative will talk with you for an hour or so and make notes on what you say. To this representative, you are just another customer; the resumé-writing service is his or her livelihood. The representative will write down what you said, add a few fancy words and printing features, and give you back "you" on paper. Some services even advertise that they will write your resumé while you wait. Considering the time you have spent on your education and work experience, could you put these things on paper in such a manner as to completely depict yourself in thirty minutes or so? To do justice to yourself and your credentials, write your own resumé. After all, you'll be called upon to defend what you put down in another phase of the job search, the interview.

Writing your own resumé is not at all difficult. You have all the information you need and you know it better than anyone else. If you follow a structured process to record all that information on paper, the job of writing your own resumé will be less overwhelming.

The first step in the preparation of your resumé is to determine what is available to put on paper. The primary tool for this step is the Personal Assessment Sheet (PAS). The PAS is a total inventory of your personal history, your educational achievements, and your work experience; all the information included on these sheets should represent the complete you. In completing the PAS, be sure to include all information. Don't be too quick to judge any information as unimportant or irrelevant. You can make that decision when you begin writing the resumé. One more word of caution: Don't be too quick to say that any piece of information sounds like boasting. When you're writing the resumé, I'll give you some guidelines that will help you decide what should and should not be included, along with an explanation.

You may think that the PAS is too time-consuming; since you already know everything about yourself, it is a useless tool. Still, completing the PAS, you will have a chance to review all your credentials and to record them in a structured manner. The PAS will not only serve as a review, but it will prepare you better for your interviews. Keep in mind that your credentials, as listed on your resumé, will be the basis for the interview later in the process. Another advantage of the PAS is that some companies will ask you to fill out an application, even though you have already submitted a resumé. If you have a copy of your PAS with you, you are sure to write consistent information on the application. This aspect is crucial to a successful job search. You would be surprised at how often I have asked an applicant to complete an application, and when I compared it with the information that was listed on the resumé, I found significant differences. Finally, because the PAS allows you to put all available data in a structured format the actual preparation of your resumé will be easier.

The Personal Assessment Sheet

The Personal Assessment Sheet is divided into three worksheets: Worksheet #1, Personal Information; Worksheet #2, Educational Data; and Worksheet #3, Work Experience. This book includes samples of these worksheets, followed by line-by-line instructions on how to complete them. Keep in mind all the advantages of using the worksheets and don't sell yourself short. The PAS may mean the difference between a job and a career. At this point, it is all up to you.

Personal Information

The Personal Information Worksheet allows you to record all your personal information. It creates a broader picture that makes you, the applicant, more visible to the employer. The following is a line-by-line description of what to record on this worksheet:

(1) Always use your legal name on your resumé. Many people have acquired nicknames which might be totally acceptable for a social event but not for the business world. Your name, like it or not, is the beginning of your professional image. Don't use Liz for Elizabeth or Bobby for Robert. Nicknames, if appropriate, will come after you have joined the organization. Keep your job search on a business-like level during the job search; your name is an excellent place to start.

(2) Your address is very important. Most companies will mail your job offer as a confirmation after your interviews and after a verbal offer of employment has been been made. It is essential that your address be correct so as not to interrupt the prospect of employment. If you live at home while attending college, you will want to use your permanent address. If you are living away from home while in school you may want to use either your home address or your school address. You may even decide to use both: this is acceptable. In fact, if a vacation from school comes up during your job search and you will be away from school for an extended period, I suggest that you use both. It can't hurt and assures that you can always be reached by mail.

(3) The telephone is probably the most essential tool for conducting business, and the well-planned job search can certainly be considered as business. The telephone number is crucial because most recruiting is done over the phone, at least in the initial stages. Use the number that gives the easiest access to you, with the possible exception of a current employer's telephone number. If your current employment is college-related, however, it may be all right to include that number. In other words, if you work at the college bookstore or other student-related establishment, your employer knows that you don't plan to make that job your career. If this is the case, make sure your employer knows that you are seeking a permanent position and ask if it's all right to be contacted there by prospective employers. Make sure you explain to the recruiter where this number is, so that everything will be clear before the phone call is made. Also, be sure your current employer understands that you will be receiving phone calls from prospective employers. In any case, always include the area code.

(4) This line is self-explanatory, though it is not necessary to include your date of birth. If you have no work experience and are seeking employment immediately after school, then list your age. It may present your lack of experience in a more sympathetic light. On the other hand, if you have some limited or advanced experience, your birth date or age could cause some concern that you are too aggressive for this particular company; more important, it could cast doubt on your entire candidacy because you couldn't possibly be so young and still able to accomplish all that you wrote on your resumé. Believe me, personnel managers look at resumés in that light.

(5) Here you must be totally honest both with yourself and with the recruiter. Don't jump too quickly onto a plane for Grand Horizons because you think it would be great to live there. Analyze your ability to start over in a strange town without long-time friends or family. Ask yourself if you're willing to meet new people and seek new activities, possibly by yourself. Your transfer to a town where you have no family or friends may call for significant adjustments and you must be willing to make those adjustments to be successful. If you don't want to transfer to this type of environment, don't accept a position that asks you to do so. It will only make your career suffer.

(6) This question gives you a chance to tell prospective employers where you want or don't want to live. It is best to place your limitations by regions, such as southwest or northeast. You may need to do some homework to find out where the company has other facilities, and consider whether or not you would like to live in those places. If you have definitely ruled out certain regions regardless of what positions are available there, don't be afraid to list those areas as unacceptable. By restricting yourself you may be ruling yourself out of consideration for some positions, but if you have decided you don't want to live in a place, no job would enhance that area as a place to live. While this question on the PAS gives you a chance to dream, it also forces you to consider the future. As I have said before, you must be totally honest to conduct a successful job search.

(7) If you have little or no job experience, this question is an opportunity to fill the gap and let your interviewer know that you haven't spent all of your free time sitting in front of the television. Employers are looking for well-rounded and well-qualified employees. List all of your interests and hobbies, regardless of how much or how little time you spend doing them. Don't feel that some of your activities are not worth mentioning because the interviewer may not be interested. The interviewer's interest is not your concern. Employers realize that a college student doesn't have much free time, but you need to show some interests outside of your studies and school activities.

Personal Information Worksheet

1. NAME:_____

2. ADDRESS: Permanent: _____

                              _____

              Temporary: _____

                              _____

3. TELEPHONE: Permanent: _____

              Temporary: _____

4. BIRTH DATE:_____

5. RELOCATABLE?_____

6. REGIONAL RESTRICTIONS:_____

7. HOBBIES OR INTERESTS:_____

   _____

8. MEMBERSHIPS IN CIVIC ORGANIZATIONS:_____

   _____

   _____

9. WHAT LANGUAGES DO YOU SPEAK?_____

   _____

10. ARE YOU BONDABLE?_____

11. HAVE YOU EVER BEEN CONVICTED OF A CRIME?:_____

12. MARITAL STATUS:_____

13. HOW MANY DAYS DID YOU MISS FROM SCHOOL OR WORK DURING THE LAST YEAR?_____

   _____

14. MILITARY STATUS:_____

15. PERSONAL REFERENCE: Name_____

                          Address_____

                          _____

16. ADDITIONAL COMMENTS:_____

   _____

(8) This is an important area. It gives you a chance to show your involvement as well as any leadership qualities you have been able to demonstrate by holding offices in the organizations to which you belong. If one of your organizations is a professional society, your membership may have enhanced professional skills that relate to your career goals. When listing the organizations, don't worry about the nature of the groups as long as they are legal. Remember to write down the nature of each organization; some are not well known, and the interviewer may not see the merit of your membership. A description may be necessary unless it is a nationally recognized organization such as Jaycees, Rotary, or Phi Beta Kappa.

(9) This may be important, especially if the prospective employer has international operations or operations near the United States border. It is important that you state honestly your proficiency in speaking and understanding the second language. Some companies will give a proficiency test as a part of the interviewing process if the second language is necessary to secure the position. Don't try to bluff your way through; bluffing will catch up with you and cause embarrassment to you and to the company. If you feel that you need to brush up on your skills, several organizations or taped courses will help you for a very small fee.

(10) This could be a requirement for a position involving financial trust. Some applicants, realizing that bonding may be necessary, investigate all the necessary requirements and execute all the necessary papers before beginning their job search. The laws on bonding vary from state to state and county to county, so I suggest that you check with the proper authorities in the area where you are seeking employment. If you are not bondable for some reason, you should either seek to correct the situation or not apply for positions that would require a bond. This action will save embarrassment to you and to the company. If you aren't really sure whether you are bondable, check with the local authorities where you are seeking employment for a list of requirements.

(11) This question will be worded in various ways, depending on the company to which you are applying. It is always worded to comply with the legal requirements of that state and of the federal government. Read the question carefully and answer it in the manner that they request. Often the application will have an "excluding clause" that allows you to omit some convictions that occurred before you reached the age of majority in the state. If the question allows you to omit certain convictions, by all means exclude them.

(12) Your marital status can be an asset or a liability, depending on the position you are seeking and the company to which you are applying. If you're applying for a position that will require a large amount of travel or out-of-town training, the company may be reluctant to hire you if you have only been married a short time. On the other hand, if the position requires some social contact in a corporate environment, being single may not enhance your image in the eyes of the company. The subject may not come up during the interview, but if it does you will have the opportunity to correct any misgivings that the interviewer may express. This particular question may sound strange, but like it or not, it is a part of the business environment. If you think your marital status might affect your chances for an interview, your best bet is to omit it from your resumé. Keep in mind that the resumé is the tool you use to get the interview, and you should not include anything on the resumé that might be considered a negative factor and prevent you from getting that first interview. Once you begin the interview, you will have the opportunity to clear up any questions.

(13) Sometimes this question is found on the application for employment. I have included it on the PAS so that you will give it some thought. It may be discussed during the interview as well. If you had many absences from school or work, you should be prepared to explain the reasons. If the absences can be attributed to unusual circumstances, the interviewer will understand them, but you must be honest. If will do you no good to try to cover them up because the interviewer will find out about them when making reference checks.

(14) This line is self-explanatory. If you are a military veteran, by all means say so here. Many companies acknowledge military service and offer preferential treatment in hiring, sometimes because of federal incentive programs to hire veterans. If you received any discharge other than honorable, such as medical or "early out," be prepared to explain the circumstances. If you have any military documentation that gives a clear picture of the circumstances, you may want to make several copies to leave with the interviewer at your first interview. This action will present the facts openly and give you an opportunity to resolve the issue face to face with the interviewer.

(15) On your resumé, you will either list your references or simply state that they are available upon request. When you are asked to complete an application for employment, however, you must be prepared to list them. On the PAS, list three references, giving accurate names, titles (if appropriate), and complete addresses and employment phone numbers. Select your references carefully from people who know you well. If you list someone who doesn't know you well, chances are the reference will tell the interviewer the extent of his or her knowledge about you. Then the interviewer will question your reason for including that name. Always ask permission of the persons you would like to use as references. This is only professional courtesy. In addition, if they have been desired ahead of time, your references will have a chance to think about what they will say to the interviewer when contacted, so that their thoughts are organized and well stated.

(16) This section allows you to make any notes of things you feel may be important for inclusion on your resumé; after all, this is a personal recap for you. Use this space if you need it. You can also use it to write down any questions you may have regarding the information you have recorded in this section of the PAS. You may need to check some of the answers to ensure accuracy. Inaccurate information could cost you the job you want.

Educational Data Worksheet

High School Data:

1. NAME AND ADDRESS OF HIGH SCHOOL:_____

    _____

    _____

2. YEARS ATTENDED: From_____ to_____

3. FAVORITE SUBJECT:_____

4. LEAST FAVORITE SUBJECT:_____

5. CLUBS AND ORGANIZATIONS:_____

    _____

    _____

6. OFFICES HELD:_____

    _____

7. ADDITIONAL COMMENTS:_____

    _____

College Data:

8. NAME OF COLLEGE OR UNIVERSITY:_____

9. ADDRESS:_____

10. YEARS ATTENDED: From_____ to_____

11. DEGREE(S) EARNED:_____

12. DEGREE MAJOR:_____

13. DEGREE MINOR:_____

14. CLUBS AND ORGANIZATIONS:_____

    _____

15. OFFICES HELD:_____

    _____

16. ACADEMIC REFERENCE: Name_____

    Address_____

Educational Data

The second question of the PAS covers all the education or training that you have completed or are in the process of completing. Again, it is important you respond completely to this section when filling in the information. Now is not the time to be modest. Include all the information, but reserve judgment about what to include in the actual resumé.

The following is a line-by-line description of the Educational Data Worksheet:

High School Data

(1) This line is self-explanatory. When you list your high school, make sure you give the complete name: not Smith High School, but John R. Smith High School. This will not only add a degree of professionalism to your resumé, but it will also show an attention to detail which can't hurt. Those recruiters in tune to detail will certainly notice it.

When listing the school's address, make sure it is correct. A prospective employer may contact your high school for references, and failure to give the correct address may slow the process, allowing someone else to get the position.

(2) It isn't necessary to give the exact dates, however, you must be consistent throughout your resumé. Exact dates will add to the impression that you pay attention to detail, which we mentioned earlier.

(3) Your favorite course will, no doubt, be a topic of discussion during the interview, especially if you are a recent graduate with limited work experience. It is included here for that reason. Give some thought to your selection and be prepared to offer a logical explanation for your selection. Under no circumstances should you try to bluff with the recruiter simply because you think that a certain subject is what he or she wants to hear. Don't tell the recruiter that you like science because you think it will help you get the position. Recruiters are trained to spot bluffing.

(4) If you are asked during the interview about your favorite course in school, the interviewer will probably ask what your least favorite course was, and why. Again, offer a logical explanation. The interviewer will attempt to form some sort of opinion based on the two answers you give. Remember that it is the interviewer's job to get as much information from you about yourself as possible. Discrepancies without explanation are usually filled in, positively or negatively, by the recruiter. This could damage your chances for employment and leave too much to chance. Offer as much detail as possible so that the interviewer doesn't have the opportunity to fill in the blanks for you.

(5) List all the clubs and organizations you belonged to while you attended high school. Be sure that the name of each club explains the purpose of the organization. As I mentioned in the previous section, don't assume that the interviewer will know the nature of the organization. You may have to explain. The type of organization is not especially important; these memberships show that you can work with a group of people, perhaps of your own age, for a common purpose.

(6) List any office you held in the organizations mentioned above and think about your duties in these offices. I have asked this question while interviewing candidates for management positions, and have received some very detailed answers. I knew from those responses that those applicants took their duties seriously. On the other hand, when I have asked others about the duties connected with their offices, the responses showed that the applicants don't know much about the offices. These individuals were probably ineffective leaders.

(7) As on the Personal Information Worksheet, this section is for your use. Record any comments or questions that you feel may need to be reviewed before you write the resumé.

On the sample Educational Data Worksheet you will notice two sections for high school data. If you attended more than one high school, complete a section for each school. In this way you can review the development of your education both for writing your resumé and for the actual interview.

College Data

(8) This line is self-explanatory. The same guidelines apply as for the high school information.

(9) This line is also self-explanatory. Make sure you give the complete and correct address, in case the interviewer needs to correspond with the school for any reason.

(10) Record the years attended on this line. You need to record only the month and year of your attendance from the beginning until you left or graduated. If you had a break in attendance other than summer vacation, show each period in attendance.

(11) In this section, list all the degrees you earned from this college or university. Don't assume that everyone understands the initials for your degrees. Spell out what you have earned! If you earned more than one degree from the same college or university, list the most recently earned degree first. Place the year in which you earned each degree in parentheses next to the respective degree.

(12) List your major area of study. For the interview you will probably need to explain why you chose this particular field. If the area doesn't seem to match the position you are seeking, develop a sound explanation of how your studies in that area will aid you in the position for which you are applying. If necessary, contact your advisor if you haven't been out of school long and tell him or her about the position you have applied for. Ask how your field of study can help you in that type of position. Most faculty members are flattered when a former student asks for advice or help. If your advisor is not available, talk to a friend who studied in the same area. Regardless of what you have to do, you must develop some reason.

A reason is not to be confused with bluffing. *Never* try to bluff, even if you have to admit that your area of study is not directly related to the position you want. The mere fact that you went to college taught you to budget time, meet deadlines and follow a planned path to obtain your degree.

(13) For this line, follow the same guidelines as you did for your major area of study. In the interview you may be asked the relationship between your major and minor areas, but it is certainly no disadvantage if they are not closely related. In fact, it may show the recruiter that you have a wide range of interests if the major and minor are on two different ends of the spectrum. The interviewer simply wants to know if you were working with an overall plan during your years in college.

(14) List memberships in clubs and organizations, whether they are academic, social, or professional. Record the year or years of your membership in parentheses so that when you prepare your resumé you will be able to present all information in a logical sequence. At this point, don't be selective about what you will list and what you will leave out. We will discuss this aspect of resumé writing in Chapter Three.

(15) List any offices you held in the above organization, along with the year you were elected to these offices. In this way the interviewer can keep track of what you were doing from year to year.

(16) The importance of this line cannot be overemphasized. Be very particular about your academic references. They don't have to include any of your professors or your faculty advisor. A reference can be any member of the school's administration, faculty, or staff. The only criterion is that your reference should have first-hand knowledge of your academic or leadership abilities. Perhaps in a smaller college your references could include the president, while in a larger university they might include a former professor. As a professional courtesy, never give someone's name as a reference without asking his or her permission first.

Work Experience

For the college student or the recent graduate, this section will probably be used to recap your summer employment. This is understandable because you have devoted most of your time to pursuing your college degree. Even though your work experience might be limited, don't underestimate it. Let me offer a word of caution: when you are referring to your summer employment, never say, "It was just a summer job." This statement may give the interviewer the impression that you didn't take the job seriously, and as a result, that you didn't give much effort to your duties. During the interview, treat any summer or part-time employment as if it was a full-time position.

A line-by-line review of the Work Experience Data Worksheet follows:

(1) Use the same guidelines for the name and address of your current employer as for the name and address of your college or university. Some employers never check with your school for references primarily because of the privacy rights regarding student records, but you can be sure of one thing—your places of employment will be checked. I can't imagine a reputable company hiring someone without checking references in detail, especially if you are applying for a management or supervisory position.

(2) Record your current position or title exactly as it was given to you. Be honest; don't try to puff it up. Don't let a basic issue such as honesty stand in the way of your getting a job because you overstated your position.

(3) On this line record your dates of employment. Be consistent in the way you record them; if you listed exact dates on the Personal Information and Educational Data Worksheets, record exact dates here, too. If you worked for the same employer in the same position during each school year and left that employment only to return home from the summer, you need to list this employer only once. If you had several positions with that employer over a number of years, however, list them separately. This should show the interviewer that your employer thought highly of your skills and allowed you to train in different positions.

(4) Here is your chance to sell yourself! Describe exactly what your duties were. Emphasize those duties that allowed you an opportunity to use independent judgment or other supervisory skills. Here you should keep in mind that a supervisor or manager has the responsibility to plan, organize, staff, direct, and control. (For a more detailed explanation of these management functions, consult any management textbook.) Use these basic functions to help interpret your duties. Don't be modest about your responsibilities. Record your duties as they were, and don't worry about the wording until you write the resumé.

(5) Record the number of hours you worked per week. If there is a wide variation in the numbers, average the hours and use that figure. Be careful: this information is a double-edged sword. If you record a great many hours and the interviewer learns you have a low grade-point average, you may have to explain why. If the number of hours is low, however, and you have an acceptable grade-point average, then the interviewer will know you were able to balance studies and work.

(6) List the favorite aspects of your position because you will probably be asked about them during the interview. The position you are seeking, you hope, has some of these characteristics. This subject will interest the interviewer as he or she tries

Work Experience Worksheet

1. NAME AND ADDRESS OF CURRENT EMPLOYER:_____

    _____

    _____

2. CURRENT POSITION:_____

3. DATES OF EMPLOYMENT: From:_____ to_____

4. DUTIES AND RESPONSIBILITIES:_____

    _____

    _____

    _____

    _____

    _____

5. AVERAGE NUMBER OF WORK HOURS PER WEEK:_____

6. FAVORITE ASPECTS OF POSITION:_____

    _____

    _____

7. LEAST FAVORITE ASPECTS OF POSITION:_____

    _____

    _____

8. BUSINESS REFERENCES: Name_____

    Address_____

    _____

    Name_____

    Address_____

    _____

9. ADDITIONAL COMMENTS:_____

    _____

    _____

to match your interests with the available position. The company doesn't want to put someone who doesn't like to work with people, for example, in a public relations position.

(7) Now list the least favorite aspects of your position. When you have done this, it may be a good time to evaluate the job you are currently seeking. Forget the salary offered or the fact that this is a full-time position; analyze the various aspects of the job and see how they compare with your part-time jobs. You may discover that you need to reconsider your career objectives and seek a job that presents a more desirable challenge. If you have any doubts, seek out someone who has a similar position in another company or even the company to which you are applying. This could help you in mapping out your career path and prevent you from making a mistake.

(8) As with your personal and education references, you must choose your business references carefully. One question to consider is whether you can use your current employer. If your current employer knows that you will be seeking other employment after you complete your education, he or she should be willing to give you a reference. (Many companies, however, will not contact current employers even if the applicant grants permission because they don't want to jeopardize the applicant's present employment.) Let the recruiter know that your employer expects to lose you when you graduate and that he or she has agreed to give you a reference. You must convince the interviewer that it is all right to contact the employer. Make sure you ask your employer whether he or she can be contacted for a reference, and then confirm this agreement when you have used the employer's name with a prospective employer. This will serve as a reminder so that he or she will be prepared when contacted.

(9) Use this section to record any other aspects of your employment that have not been covered on the worksheet. If your employer gave you special training or enrolled you in outside training classes, record that information in this section.

You should fill out a Work Experience Data Worksheet for every job you have held during your career. Some jobs may require you to record more information, but it is important that you put all the facts on paper. When you write the resumé, you will discard some of the information, but you still may need it for employment applications.

Once you have completed all worksheets for the Personal Assessment Sheets, put them away for a few days and then review them. You may have thought of other items that should be included, or you may have to correct some of the information you have already included. If you made notes of things that needed to be checked, check before you start to write the resumé.

If you are certain that all the information is complete and correct, it is time to move to the next phase of your job search—the writing of the resumé. Don't give up now; the worst part of the resumé writing is over. You now have all the material you need to make the best possible presentation of your credentials. Now all you have to do is organize it in a professional format.

CHAPTER THREE

The Resumé

The resumé is the most common tool used in the job search process today, except for the direct application for employment. This has not always been the case, however. In the past the resumé was used primarily by white-collar applicants seeking employment in professional positions at the higher levels of an organization. Today, resumés are used by all levels of the work force to apply for all kinds of positions.

The resumé is your method of advertising yourself and your credentials as you conduct your job search and put your career plans in motion. From the very beginning of planning your career I have stressed the need to sell yourself, and the resumé is the way to accomplish that. To state it in sales terms the resumé is the brochure that advertises your product, which is you, the applicant. In this brochure, you should list all the specifications that describe the product fully. The resumé is a composite of you, the applicant, on paper. You must present personal information along with your educational data and work experience in such a manner as to give the best possible picture of you and to show logical progress to this point in your life. Resumés that contain the most pertinent information about the applicant's personal life, education, and work history as related to the available position have the best chance of being read by the personnel manager.

The information in a resumé must be presented in such a manner as to encourage more contact with the employer, so that a more detailed discussion can take place between the applicant and the personnel manager. To aid in this process, the information must be easy to follow and illustrate your accomplishments clearly whether in your education or in your work experience. A personnel manager does not want to wade through a mound of papers to decipher a candidate's qualifications. He or she would rather see a clear picture of the qualifications in a concise, structured manner which can be reviewed easily in less than three minutes. Remember, the personnel manager probably receives many resumés within a month's time and many more in answer to a want ad. I once ran an ad for a management position in a small town and received more than two hundred resumés from interested applicants.

Depending on the type of position, the average resumé is reviewed in about three minutes. Resumés that cannot pass screening during that time are either passed over or discarded. I personally don't have longer than three minutes to read an applicant's credentials. Even if you are the most qualified candidate for a position, your chances are slim if your resumé can't be deciphered or if it isn't read at all because of length or content. Would you buy a product if you couldn't read or understand the label or the instructions? I don't think so. By using a structured format, you can avoid this problem from the very beginning.

Types of Resumés

Many types of resumés are being used in the job market today. The type generally depends on many factors, including personal preference, the type of position sought, the degree of work experience, and the area chosen for career plans. For our purposes we will deal with the two basic types of resumés: the chronological and the functional. These two types will serve our purpose primarily for two reasons: 1) as a college student, your educational activities probably represent your greatest accomplishments to date; and 2) your work experience, if any, may add little or nothing to your chosen career. This is not to say that your work experience has been of no benefit to you in terms of seeking employment. Even if it doesn't exactly complement your chosen career path, it will still demonstrate your desire to achieve a goal through part-time employment regardless of the job itself. If you have been fortunate enough to obtain part-time employment in your chosen field, these two types of resumés will allow you to focus on both your education and your work experience.

To explain the two types of resumés, let's take a look at each of them.

The Chronological Resumé

The chronological resumé lists all education, work experience, extracurricular activities, and awards in chronological order. One variation is to list all the data in reverse order, with your most current degree, job, activities, and awards second, and so on.

19

The chronological resumé is easiest for someone who wants to follow your educational and career development. It will greatly reduce the need for "translation."

The Functional Resumé

The functional resumé emphasizes your qualifications and abilities in terms of previous job titles and responsibilities. In this type of resumé, dates are usually not listed and no logical progression of your career can be seen. When I am reviewing resumés, I look for both dates and logical progression. They give me an indication of what the applicant has done in the past and what efforts he or she has made to begin career development. Without dates, I feel that something is missing, and sometimes I become frustrated at not knowing when certain things happened in the applicant's life. Remember that as personnel manager, I am charged with the responsibility of recruiting the most qualified employees to mesh with the current work force and with company goals. To do this, I must know as much as possible about the candidates. Without the dates I can't get a clear picture of the logical progression and I am reluctant to hire the candidate.

The functional resumé does allow you to broaden your "brochure" by letting you describe the responsibilities in several of your part-time jobs to develop a more detailed "experience" section. If you have had positions that fit your career path, you may want to use the functional resumé. For this reason, I have included it in this book.

After you have reviewed the samples of both the chronological and the functional resumé, you should be able to decide which is best for you. If you can't decide, you may want to try writing both. In this way you may find that your first choice wasn't really the right one.

Sample Chronological Resumé

RONALD EUGENE WATSON

PERMANENT: 2430 Crockett Drive   PRESENT: 1950 Mosby Drive
            Marietta, Georgia 30307   Athens, Georgia 35412
            (404) 999-3354   (404) 467-8205

OBJECTIVE: To obtain an entry level position leading to a senior governmental auditor.

EDUCATION:

September, 1974 to June, 1978   Hardaway High School, College Drive
                                             Columbus, Georgia 31985
                                             Diploma

September, 1978 to June, 1982   University of Georgia, First Avenue
                                             Athens, Georgia 35412
                                             Bachelor of Science Degree
                                             Major: Accounting; Minor: Finance

EXPERIENCE:

January, 1981 to present   Lawson, Bowers and Herring Accounting
                                             817 Macon Drive
                                             Athens, Georgia 35412
                                             Audit Intern

                                             Assisted audit team in conducting corporate
                                             audits for private clients by performing research,
                                             analysis and drafting preliminary reports for
                                             senior auditor review.

June, 1979 to September, 1979   Cobb County Parks and Recreation Dept.
                                             1121 Lower Roswell Road
                                             Marietta, Georgia 30306

                                             Planned and scheduled activities for 300 youth
                                             during summer recreation program. Filed activity
                                             reports for county director and assisted in
                                             completing grant requests from state agency.

ACTIVITIES AND AWARDS:

Phi Beta Kappa, 1982; Varsity baseball, 1982; *Who's Who in American Colleges*, 1982; *Outstanding Young Men of America*, 1981; Pilot Club, 1980.

PERSONAL DATA:

Single, bondable, willing to relocate.
References available upon request.

Sample Chronological Resumé

Vanessa Dale Smith
817 Village Lane
Harrisonburg, Virginia 22801

OBJECTIVE

To obtain a position in a public organization involved in national economic development.

EDUCATION

Bachelor of Arts Degree, George Washington University, Washington. D.C. 20202.

EXPERIENCE

National Affairs Intern, Department of Energy, Office of National Affairs, Washington, D.C.

Assisted in researching, analyzing and preparing proposals on local energy conditions in underdeveloped regions of the United States. Conducted onsite inspections of targeted areas while conducting surveys of needs of area residents. Drafted summaries for agency review and costing. (1981-1983)

Volunteer, Volunteer In Service To America (VISTA), Washington, D.C.

Provided assistance to underdeveloped areas in United States in the areas of agriculture and construction. Teamed with group of eight other volunteers in the construction of schools in the isolated sections of the Blue Ridge Mountain region while also establishing local agriculture centers to promoted self-sufficiency. (1970)

Assistant Recreation Coordinator, Rockingham County Parks and Recreation, Harrisonburg, Virginia.

Assisted recreation coordinator in the daily activities for underprivileged children. Maintain participation records of all children ages 6 to 14 for grant proposals as well as future planning for the recreation department budgets. (1979)

PERSONAL DATA

Single, open to travel, willing to relocate to any region of the United States. Able to read and speak Spanish fluently.

References Available Upon Request

Sample Functional Resumé

MARTHALYN WALKER

Permanent: 1672 Wellington Drive
Arlington, Virginia 22004
(703) 464-6212

Temporary: 5690 Kenmore Lane
Atlanta, Georgia 30030
(404) 267-8970

EXPERIENCE

NEWS

Production Assistant Intern, Turner Broadcasting, Inc., Atlanta, Georgia
Investigative researcher, assistant video editor, camera technician for state governmental agency hearings.

Television News Monitor, Cox Broadcasting, Atlanta, Georgia
Logged and recorded content analysis of state newscasts for editorial staff.

RESEARCH

Legal Researcher, Walker, Dobson, and Major Law Firm, Conyers, Georgia
Investigated and researched proposed legislation in the area of child abuse.

Legislative Intern, United States Senate, Office of Herman Talmadge, Washington, D.C.
Attended Senate Committee Hearings on Agriculture and researched proposed legislation affecting Georgia agriculture.

MANAGEMENT

Student Government President, Georgia State University, Atlanta, Georgia
Planned and coordinated all student activities while representing the student body to the Administrative Committee of the University. Maintained annual budget of $93,000 dollars.

EDUCATION

Georgia State University, Atlanta, Georgia
Bachelor of Arts Degree, Broadcast Journalism. Concentration in Communication, Speech. Graduate courses: Telecommunication Systems, Telecommunication Concepts.

References Available Upon Request.

CHAPTER FOUR

Writing That Resumé!

Once you have decided which resumé you plan to use, you can begin actually writing the resumé. Many people regard writing the resumé as an unpleasant task simply because they don't feel comfortable in writing concisely about themselves and speaking only of the positive things. Most people would find it easier to write a short autobiography with no restrictions on detail or length, but unfortunately there isn't a personnel manager west of New York City who has the time to read a twenty-page summary of every person applying for a position with their company. Remember, you are aiming for a finished product that will not exceed two pages with plenty of margin space. Ideally, the finished resumé is only one page long unless you have had an exceptional amount of employment that has contributed directly to your chosen career. Remember, now is not the time to be modest. Describe yourself and your educational and work experience as if you were a third-party bystander.

The resumé, regardless of type, includes six different sections. When combined on paper, these should give a true composite picture of you and present you in the best possible light to the personnel manager or recruiter. These six sections are as follows:

1. Personal Data
2. Career Objective
3. Educational Data
4. Work Experience
5. Activities and Awards
6. Miscellaneous Data

As we review each of the six sections, we will illustrate the various types of information that you should include and mention those items that you could include. I said in Chapter Two, now is the time to decide what to include in your resumé.

Let me add a word of caution: make sure your resumé is a composite of your credentials and not a creation of credentials. Some people have enjoyed the resumé-writing portion of the job search because it gave them an opportunity to do some creative writing. Don't be guilty of overselling yourself to the point that you can't live up to your employer's expectations. This is usually called "puffing," and while puffing may get you a job, you may have trouble keeping it. This is the worst thing you can do in starting a new career. It could haunt you for a long time, especially when your references are checked for future employment. You would have to explain to future prospective employers exactly what happened and you and your career may not be able to overcome this obstacle. The simplest way to prevent this disaster is to include only totally true information in your resumé.

Now let's review each section.

1. Personal Data:

This section of the resumé consists of personal information such as your full name, address, and telephone number. If you are a student living away from home, you may want to list both your school address and your home address. If you decide to list only one address, position it in the top right-hand corner of the page. This position is important because it is considered the most readable part of the page. If you use both addresses, position the permanent address in the top left-hand corner with appropriate margins. Make sure that your margins are set so as to allow enough space for the personnel manager or interviewer to write notes on the page. Don't use any abbreviations in this portion of the resumé, and always use zip codes and area codes. Here is an example of the personal data entry for your resumé.

John Lee Applicant	John Lee Applicant
1200 Smith Road	123 First Avenue
Hometown, Georgia 30303	University, Virginia 20202
(404) 765-4321	(703) 123-4567

These examples illustrate how you should present the personal data on the top of your resumé. They should show which is your permanent address and which is your temporary address, if you find it necessary to use both. If you think the personnel manager may not know which address you consider more accessible, then you should label them. Note the example:

Permanent:	John Lee Applicant 1200 Smith Road Hometown, Georgia 30303 (404) 765-4321	Temporary:	John Lee Applicant 123 First Avenue University, Virginia 30303 (703) 123-4567

You can use either of these two examples. If you decide not to use the labels for the addresses, you can make the distinction in the cover letter that you will attach to your resumé in some cases. Whichever method you decide to use, make sure the personnel manager knows how to get in touch with you. Because most job searches are conducted at first primarily over the phone, you will also want to let the personnel manager know which telephone number to use.

2. Career Objective

Your career objective is a broad statement about your career choice and what career path you would like to follow to gain your planned position in the next five years. When writing your objective you should include in some manner the position that you are currently seeking. In stating the objective, show the planned position and how your present position progresses naturally to the planned one. In addition, you may want to draw the personnel manager's attention to some credential that you feel will greatly enhance your ability to perform the job for the employer. The following are examples of career objectives:

"To seek an entry-level position in data processing that will allow advancement to the position of computer programmer."

"To obtain an entry-level management position in the insurance industry which will allow me to advance to middle management, where I can use my human relations skills."

"To obtain a position in marketing, leading to increased responsibility as department manager."

"To obtain a position in personnel where I can use my personnel management degree and my human relations skills."

Your career objective should combine your career plans and your personal strengths and focus them in light of the company's needs. If you take the time to develop an effective career objective, your resumé writing will be much easier. Without the objective it will be difficult to focus your resumé credentials toward a specific job.

The wording of your objective is very important. Focus your statement so that it has a natural relationship to the position for which you are applying. It should reflect what you would like to do for the next three to five years or perhaps even longer, depending on your chosen career.

3. Educational Data

This section is probably the focal point of your resumé because you have spent most of your time in pursuing your education. Provide as much pertinent information as possible. Include such items as dates, name of college or university, school address, major subject, and minor subject. Many personnel people have mixed opinions about including the grade-point average, whatever it may be. Some believe that you should include it if it is at least a 3.00 on a 4.00 scale. I think this decision depends on your chosen career and the company that you are interviewing with. Not all companies are impressed by a high grade-point average. You will have to make this decision for yourself.

The placement of the educational data on your resumé is important, and must present a uniform appearance. People have a tendency to reject disorderly-looking products. Make sure the format you use is consistent throughout; it should be compatible with your work experience. I personally prefer the block method format for the chronological resumé.

Begin with the date at the left margin of the page. Apply the same rule about dates to the resumé to the preparation of your Personal Assessment Sheet. Above all, be consistent in recording dates to aid in the uniform presentation of all your credentials. If you start with the month and year, follow this format throughout the resumé. If you have only a little work experience, it is best to list only the month and year to remove the emphasis from your lack of long service. In this case you should also list the month and year when recording educational data. As you gain more experience and more time in the work force, specific dates will become less important.

The following is a sample of an educational entry.

September, 1968 to June, 1972   Georgia State University
University Plaza, Atlanta, GA
30301. Bachelor of Arts Degree.
Major: Political Science
Minor: Sociology

Be consistent as well in the use of semicolons, colons, underlining, and periods.

If you have not yet received your degree, it is proper to list the expected date of graduation if you are currently enrolled or to list the total number of academic hours you have earned toward your degree if you are not currently enrolled in classes. If you have just started work on your degree and have been attending school part time, don't give a completion date if it is more than a year away. Any period longer than that could be a negative feature. Don't give the person who reads the resumé a chance to make a quick value judgment about how long it will take you to complete your degree.

Finally, remember to list your most recent educational data first, the next most recent data next, and so on.

If you are seeking your first full-time career job, I recommend that you list your high school data on your resumé. Record the same information about your high school as you did with your college. Give the date in month and year along with the full name of the school and the correct address. In place of a degree, enter the word "Diploma,." If you dropped out of school and received a GED, list the high school that you attended last. In place of the word "Diploma," write "GED received" along with the month and year you received it.

Continue with your entries until you have listed all the educational data from the present back to high school. If you were not in school for some period longer than the three-month summer break, you must account for that time elsewhere on your resumé.

4. Work Experience

As you consider this section of the resumé, be sure to analyze all your summer and part-time employment. Some of the skills you learned in these positions can be valuable in helping you get the position you're looking for. Make sure this section of your resumé tells the true story of your work experience. This is probably the most difficult part of the resumé to write because you must tell about yourself and your achievements. Remember—this is a sales tool and you have a product to sell, so sell it!

The key to this section is the appearance of achievement and accomplishment. Even if your jobs didn't offer direct experience for your chosen career, your skills in leadership, organization, or development can all be helpful credentials for any position that you seek.

In addition, you must describe briefly the duties and responsibilities in your jobs that helped you develop the skills you possess. Describe your duties and responsibilities positively and enthusiastically. The use of action verbs will help here. Let that employer know that despite your age and lack of much work experience, you have done something besides go to school. Employers are impressed with the fact that you have accomplished your educational goals but still took the time to work in some type of position, regardless of your reason for working.

Listed below is a list of action verbs that you should use in preparing your resumé.

accelerated	implemented
achieved	improved
administered	increased
analyzed	inspected
applied	instructed
attained	initiated
classified	maintained
communicated	managed
compared	motivated
compiled	negotiated
conducted	operated
contacted	organized
coordinated	participated
counseled	performed
created	planned
delegated	prepared
developed	presented
directed	produced
effected	reduced
encouraged	reorganized
established	reported

evaluated	researched
expanded	supervised
expedited	trained

Action verbs will bring your activities to life and tell the interviewer that you are eager to embark on your career. The following sample entries show how you should present your work experience on your resumé:

September, 1971 to present

Herring Industries, 824 Charles Avenue
University, Virginia 20202.
Assistant Inventory Control Manager
Supervised four employees during all phases of inventory control on second shift. Responsible for maintaining automated inventory system; trained new employees on methods and procedures.

June, 1971 to August, 1971

City Recreation, 123 Park Road
Hometown, Georgia 30303
Recreation Counselor
Planned, coordinated, and supervised summer recreation activities for 300 youths ages 6 to 15. Maintained all registration and participation data. Completed all necessary paperwork for state funds program.

Complete an entry for every position that you held for any period of time. If you don't have any job-for-pay entries, think of the volunteer work you have done that helped you develop some of the skills we have mentioned. You may have planned activities as a member of a group or a civic organization, or in your own part-time business ventures. Recruiters are looking for individuals who have some experience—not necessarily at a particular job, but in the skills necessary to perform that type of job. Don't be reluctant to sell yourself by telling the interviewer, through your resumé, what skills you have acquired through all your activities. This may be the only chance you have to be invited for an interview. Without the interview, you don't get the job.

5. Activities and Awards

In this section, prepare a listing of all the activities in which you have been involved, in which membership was not based strictly on popularity. List any fraternity or sorority membership (social and professional) and any club or organization that promotes educational, professional, or social activities.

When you list any activity or organization, also give the year or years of your participation. Follow the format of listing the most recent events first, and list the activities in descending order by year of participation.

When recording the activity, make sure the name of the activity or organization is self-explanatory. If it is not, explain the nature of the organization in parentheses.

Many job seekers have asked me how many organizations or other memberships should be listed. This is a difficult question, but you should try to keep a balance between education, work, and outside activities. If your academic performance is good and you also have a part-time job, the interviewer knows you don't have much free time. On the other hand, if you have a long list of activities which are mainly socially oriented, be selective about which ones to list if you have no work experience. Remember, employers are looking for well-rounded individuals, so try to present your credentials to depict you as that type of person.

The method that you use in placing your activities and awards on your resumé is a matter of form and personal preference. It isn't necessary to stick to the block format that we have used up to this point. By placing this information in line form, you can add some variation to the final version. In writing your rough draft, you may want to try several methods to see which one you prefer.

Here are some samples of activities and organizations entries, using various formats:

(block style)
Activities and Awards:

Student Government Association, senator, 1969-72; *Who's Who in American Colleges*, 1972; college newspaper, editor, 1971; Sigma Alpha Epsilon Fraternity, 1971-72; debate team, 1969.

(list style)

Activities and Awards:	Student Government Association, senator, 1969-72
	Who's Who in American Colleges, 1972
	College newspaper, editor, 1971
	Sigma Alpha Epsilon Fraternity, 1971-73
	Debate team, 1969

(line style)

Activities and Awards: Student Government Association, senator, 1969-72; *Who's Who in American Colleges*, 1972; college newspaper, editor, 1971; Sigma Alpha Epsilon Fraternity, 1971-72; debate team, 1969.

6. Miscellaneous Data

In this section of the resumé, include data listed on your personal information worksheet as a part of the PAS, such as hobbies, interests, willingness to relocate, foreign language skills, bondability, marital status (optional), number of dependents (optional), and availability of references.

I recommend that you use the line form in entering this information on your resumé. The list form will give a very formal look to the resumé, but this is personal, not professional information. Here is an example of the line form:

Miscellaneous Data: Interested in historical sightseeing, golf; open to relocation in southeast; speak and write Spanish fluently; single. References available upon request.

As you begin your first draft of the resumé, make sure you have placed each section so as to present a uniform but attractive document. The appearance of the resumé is very important to the success of your job search. Keep trying the various formats or combinations until you find one that looks good to you. It is your sales tool, and you should be proud of it.

Now that we have reviewed the six sections of the resumé, we need to consider how to put it into final form so that you can proceed with your job search. Read the next section carefully.

Presenting the Resumé

When you have decided on the contents, it's time to consider how to present them in their final form. Some people fail to pay enough attention to this area, not realizing that a resumé that looks less than professional will probably undo any other efforts they have made in their job search. Please don't think that I'm overstating the importance of presentation. I have received many more resumés than I care to admit that didn't meet business standards. They contained misspelled words, incomplete information, incomplete addresses, and misuse of punctuation. Worst of all, my name was spelled incorrectly. This is totally unacceptable in the job market. Make sure your resumé meets all acceptable standards—in other words, make sure it is letter perfect before you distribute it to anyone.

Typing versus Printing

Perhaps it is unrealistic to think that you will be able to type a fresh resumé for every prospective employer or every personnel agency. I must agree. If you have to spend all your time or money to have a fresh resumé typed every time you need one, you will be worn out before you have acquired the job of your choice. I suggest that you have your resumé printed after it has been typed and the layout is perfect.

When typing your resumé, use an electric or electronic typewriter with a carbon ribbon. The IBM Selectric or Panasonic Electronic are excellent typewriters to type the resumé before having it printed. Liquid erasures have a tendency to show up when you copy the resumé so make sure you have a typewriter with a correction ribbon.

Once you have completed the typing, take it to an "instant copier" company. they will normally print it by using the offset method, which is the cheapest way today to have something printed. In this process, the printer takes a picture of the original typed resumé. A printing plate is made from this picture, and all your printing is done from the plate. The result is professional-looking copies of your resumé, which will enhance your professional image. Be careful in typing your final resumé because the picture for the plate will show all the marks on the paper.

Selection of Paper

The paper is just as important as the printing. Follow standard business practices. This is not the time to pick your favorite color—save that for decorating your new apartment. Stick to traditional high-quality white paper. A friend of mine once had his resumé printed on a light gray paper with black ink which is a slight variation of the standard white paper with black ink.

Ink

Always use traditional black ink. Regardless of the paper color, black ink will show up well. Any other color may reduce the clarity of the print. When choosing your paper and ink, remember that this resumé will be read by someone who probably spends a great deal of time reading resumés. A picture of an excellent resumé sticks with the reader, but any great deviation from the business norm will stand out in an unfavorable way. It isn't worth the risk; play it safe with your selections.

Envelopes

Your envelopes should be the same color and quality as the paper you selected for the resume. Don't send your sales tool in anything less than a professional wrapper. You would be surprised at the number of resumés I receive enclosed in dingy white envelopes stained with coffee. When you have the resumé printed, ask the printer if he has envelopes to match the paper. The availability of matching envelopes my help you make your final decision as to which paper to use.

Now that you have the completed product in your hand, it is time to start the advertising phase. That is the job search itself.

CHAPTER FIVE

The Job Selection

To some people, job selection is the most enjoyable part of the job search process. During this phase the applicant has the chance to shop through the job market and select the type of job and the company that he or she plans to pursue. As you shop, you will be able to conduct a survey of what companies are currently hiring, what positions, and what benefit packages are most attractive to a new person in the job market. In other words, you will take a complete inventory of the employment picture, both for your career plans and for the place where you would like to live.

The availability of information for this inventory depends on how much time and effort you want to put into it. You will have many sources of information about the job market, but some will be more readily available than others. The following is a list of possible sources, with a brief comment about each. If you have other sources, by all means use them. There is no rule about where to find a job. Use these sources or any others that are available to you.

Newspaper classified advertisements

Many people use this source as their main avenue in conducting their job search, even though only 20 percent of all positions ever appear in newspaper advertisements. This figure should not discourage you, however. You can find valuable information in these ads.

The weekend editions of the newspapers, especially the larger cities, contain the most employment ads and usually give the most detailed and helpful information. If you are living away from the city while going to school, you can subscribe to the weekend editions. Allowing for time in the mail, you should have the information by the following Tuesday. The short delay shouldn't delay your search long, and the information should still be accurate. Positions aren't generally filled in only a few days.

The information in the classified ads is arranged first by major career area, such as data processing, engineering, management, or personnel. Then the information is divided alphabetically by career subsections. Under the heading of engineering, for example, you would find electrical, industrial, mechanical, and so on. The format and size of the information in each ad depends on the company placing the ad. The company has complete control over the content of the advertisement. Some companies consider the placement of ads as a chance to do some public relations work, and will place large ads that give more detailed information about the company and the position. The larger display ads are expensive, and you can generally expect this type of ad to contain information about the particular company as well as the position and benefits. Although the company may use large display ads both for recruiting and for public relations, some applicants are discouraged by the size of the ads whether large or small. If the ad is large, they feel that the competition will be too great, but if it is small, they may feel that the quality of the company is not high. Don't be guilty of this attitude. Judge the ad by the contents. Is the position advertised the type of position you would like to have? Do the benefits offered meet your financial planning needs? If a salary is stated in the advertisement, does it meet your needs for the next few years? Companies generally prefer not to include salary in the larger ad. For this reason you need to do as much research as possible about companies and positions and about the salaries offered in similar positions in the industry. You could lose valuable time if you don't know what salary range to expect from a certain type of position and if you go through two or three interviews, only to find that the salary the company is willing to pay is not enough to satisfy your needs.

State employment agencies

In most states you will find an agency operated by the state to aid in the employment of its citizens. This is often a forgotten source of employment opportunities, especially for those seeking white-collar employment. Many companies, especially new companies in an area, list positions with these agencies. New companies that are seeking a large number of employees often use the services of these agencies to conduct their hiring process quickly and smoothly. A company places "orders" for the number and types of employees needed, and an agency can place employment ads in the newspapers in the names of the agency without identifying the company. Interested candidates must register with the agency through an employment counselor, who tries in turn to match the candidate with the available positions. After the initial screening and matching are done, the counselor turns the candidates' credentials over to the personnel department of the company for further screening.

If you decide to include this source in your job selection process, a copy of your resumé and your PAS will serve to answer any questions the counselor may ask. Try to work with the same counselor each time you visit the agency, to reduce the need for repeating the information a second or third time. Remember that state agencies are there to serve all citizens of the state, and therefore have a large variety of candidates for a variety of positions. As a result, they are unable to specialize in any particular field. Some people feel that this situation creates a greater concern for placement statistics than for making placements based on a career match. Even so, if you can work with a counselor who takes a genuine interest in your employment efforts in your chosen career field, he or she can give a big boost to your job search.

Personnel agencies

Personnel agencies are one of the most popular methods used in the job search today, especially in the larger cities, where the competition for career positions is great. College students are often reluctant to use the services offered by personnel agencies because of their lack of experience in the work force and because they don't know how personnel agencies work.

Representatives at the agencies understand that a college student has very little work experience when the placement process begins, and they know how to deal with it in a manner that stresses the applicant's ability to learn and progress within an entry-level position. Often they focus on educational background and extracurricular activities, including leadership potential and other qualities.

The personnel agency acts as the applicant's agent in helping him or her match his career interest with a position he will be happy with. The representative researches the company and the position in an attempt to sell the company and the position to the applicant. This may sound somewhat confusing, but keep in mind that the company has contacted the agency as a means of recruiting. It has spelled out what type of position is available and what type of person the company feels will best meet its needs. While the representative may seem to work for the applicant, in reality he or she is working for the company. This situation creates a delicate balance; the agency representative must stay within professional boundaries.

One issue that the representative must consider is who is paying the placement fee. In some agencies the fee is paid by the applicant, while in others it is paid by the company or by a combination of both. You must decide for yourself whether you are willing to pay a fee. Some people feel that they shouldn't have to pay a placement fee, and will accept only those positions in which the employer pays. It is not unusual for the company to pay the entire fee or to make arrangements to split the fee with the applicant.

If you are planning to use an agency to help you with your job search, you must understand how the process works. Don't hesitate to ask questions about the contractual arrangements, because normally you will be asked to sign some type of contract giving the agency permission to act on your behalf. The contract generally includes a provision regarding the payment of fees if a company that doesn't pay the fee for the applicant offers a position that interests you.

The following chart will give you some idea of fees paid by the employer to a personnel agency for recruiting one person:

Annual Salary	Fee
to $9,999	10%
$10,000 to $11,999	12%
$12,000 to $12,999	13%
$13,000 to $13,999	15%
$14,000 to $15,999	16%
$16,000 to $16,999	17%
$17,000 to $17,999	18%
$18,000 to $18,999	19%
$19,000 to $19,999	20%
$20,000 to $20,999	21%
$21,000 to $21,999	22%
$22,000 to $22,999	23%
$23,000 to $23,999	24%
$24,000 to $24,999	25%
$25,000 to $25,999	26%
$26,000 to $26,999	27%
$27,000 to $27,999	28%
$28,000 to $28,999	29%

$29,000 and above	30%

The placement fee is based upon the position's total annual salary, and it becomes due and payable when the employee begins work. The fee schedule that the applicant pays is similar to this but is generally not as high. Ask for a copy of the schedule that will be used in your agreement. Don't be too quick to accept a position that will cost you a fee you don't want to pay. You don't need to deal with legal problems at the beginning of your career.

Try to deal with an agency that has a representative who deals exclusively with placements in your field. He or she can be more knowledgeable about one field than two or three. Ask the representative about his or her track record for placements in your chosen field. They should not be reluctant to share that information with you. Any hesitation should warn you to search further for a representative in whom you have more confidence.

After you have selected the agency and the representative, you will be asked to fill out an application and a reference release, which will give the agency permission to contact your references and previous employers. Usually you will be asked to sign a contract with the agency. After that you will be interviewed by the representative so that you can become more familiar with each other and a better career match can be made. The representative will work to place you, but can do so only if you have marketable skills and if there is a market for your skills. Don't expect overnight miracles or guaranteed success. The placement for some positions may take a month or longer, so don't become impatient. Success is not guaranteed just because you have registered with an agency. It would not be wise to depend exclusively on the representatives. Try to use the personnel agency's search to supplement your own.

When the representative finds a possible position, he or she will contact you and review all vital information regarding the position and the company. If you're not interested in this particular position don't hesitate to give the representative your reasons. Be as candid as possible so as not to waste your time or his. After all, it is your career, and you will have to live with it.

University Placement Office

Most colleges and universities have some type of placement office that assists the graduates of the school in acquiring employment after graduation. It operates like the personnel agency in that it maintains records of your chosen career and invites companies to the campus to review student's credentials and interview those who are interested.

Universities and colleges use placement offices to varying degrees. The placement office prepares and mails personal data about applicants to prospective employers along with letters of recommendation and a college transcript if the company has requested that type of information. Normally the placement office is used as a source of information for the job market, and operates as a service to the students and the business community. Some companies look to certain schools to provide them with graduates to fill all openings in their organization. Stay in touch with your school's placement office to learn about possible openings in your career field. It will also help you to participate in the on-campus interviews.

Other sources

Other sources are also available to you. By using every possible resource you have a greater chance for a successful job selection and can pursue every possible lead. In addition to the sources we discussed above, keep in mind that one of your best sources of information can be the people you see regularly, such as family, friends, or work associates. Ask your parents and their friends about jobs. You may be able to find employment at the same company as your parents or your friend's parents if any areas of that company offer you the opportunity you want.

Another source can be the business section of your newspapers. Watch for new companies coming into your area or the area where you plan to live after graduation. If you discover that a company is relocating or expanding, by all means pursue employment with that company by contacting other facilities of that company to learn who is in charge of staffing the newest facility.

The list of other sources could be extensive. Remember, keep your eyes and ears open to new opportunities of employment. Your diligence in seeking out sources of employment may mean the difference between getting a job and starting your chosen career.

The Cover Letter

With the list of sources you plan to pursue available, you must begin your actual job search. In some cases you will be able to hand deliver your resumé, but in others you will be conducting a portion of your job search by mail. One rule that should always be followed is, *never* mail a resumé to a prospective employer without using a cover letter.

The cover letter serves as a brief introduction for you and should be written in such a way as to create interest in your credentials and candidacy for the particular position. In addition, it should express desire on your part for the position in a way that illustrates how your qualifications can match the needs of the company. In concluding the letter, you should ask for an appointment to further discuss the position and your qualifications, while also suggesting a time when you will be free.

The cover letter should be typed and addressed to a particular individual rather than to a title or a "Dear Sir." If you are not sure of the individual that you should send it to, call the company and ask. This is not an unusual question. For an added degree of professionalism, the letter should be typed on the same letter quality paper as the resumé.

On the next two pages you will see two sample cover letters that meet acceptable business standards. Review them carefully for content and structure. An excellent cover letter can only enhance your position in the job search.

Sample Cover Letter

2418 Ramlin Way
Barnesville, Georgia 30183
January 31, 1984

Ms. Regenia Gaskin
Recruiting Manager
Tri-State Insurance, Inc.
Atlanta, Georgia 30300

Dear Ms. Gaskin:

The Placement Office at Georgia State University has given me your name as the appropriate contact for employment with Tri-State Insurance Company. I have talked with several employees of Tri-State and find their jobs in line with my qualifications and career goals, and would like to be considered for a position as claims administrator.

I am a candidate for graduation from Georgia State in June of this year with a Bachelor of Arts degree with a major in Business. My area of concentration has been Insurance and Finance which I feel would be extremely beneficial in a position as claims administrator. This background, along with my experience in meeting and interacting with people, would allow me to prove I would be an asset to your company and existing staff.

I would like to discuss my qualifications with you at your earliest convenience and would like to learn more about the employment opportunities with Tri-State Insurance. My resumé is enclosed for your review. My references are on file at the Placement Office at Georgia State. I look forward to hearing from you.

Sincerely,

Deborah Ramsey

Enclosure

Sample Cover Letter

432 Solomon Avenue
Knowville, TN 37919
April 12, 1985

Mr. John Walker
Randolph Muffler Company
1453 Dresden Street
Knoxville, TN 37918

Dear Mr. Walker:

I would like to be considered as an applicant for the management trainee position at Randolph Muffler Company. I am a candidate for graduation from James Madison University in May of this year. I like this geographical area and would like to remain here. Your company's reputation for being concerned about the growth and development of your employees is one of the main reasons I would like to begin my career here.

As you can see by the attached resumé, I have held several part-time positions while attending school that not only required me to budget my time but was able to finance over 85% of all educational expenses. The duties and responsibilities grew with each position and I always received excellent performance reviews from my employers.

I welcome the opportunity to meet with you and discuss the position and how my qualifications could benefit your comapny. I look forward to hearing from you.

Sincerely,

Rodney Harris

Enclosure

CHAPTER SIX

The Interview

The interview can be considered the finale of the job search. This is what you have been working toward since the earlier stages when you were making plans and preparing your resumé. If you have been invited for an interview, your job search has been successful to this point, but don't get too comfortable—you must still meet the challenge of the interview. You could lose all the ground you have gained if you aren't prepared for the interview. If you study this section closely, you will be prepared.

During the interview, the interviewer seeks information that will be used as part of the basis for the final selection. Keep in mind that the interviewer has all the information that you submitted earlier, by resumé or by employment application, or both. This information will be the basis of your interview, so you must be totally familiar with the contents. Through the questions asked in the interview, the interviewer will try to verify the information by asking questions that will allow you to explain yourself. Your answers will either confirm or contradict the information you submitted, and will give the interviewer insight into your ability to deal with pressure, express yourself orally, and fit the mold that the interviewer feels will be the ideal candidate. This is not to say that the interviewer knows *whom* the company wants, but the company certainly knows *what* it wants. You must fill this mold or show that, even if you don't fit it exactly, you will be able to function effectively in that position.

From the very beginning, I have talked about the absolute need to sell yourself. Your selling ability is most important of all during the interview. Until this point, your ability to sell has been confined to indirect contacts, such as telephone calls, letters of application, or resumés. During the interview, however, the situation changes. Your selling ability will be tested in face-to-face meetings. The interview is a true sales meeting between the seller (you, the applicant) and the buyer (the employer), discussing the buyer's needs and the product offered. The recruiter will try to determine your ability to fill the position and to fit into the organization, while you try to convince the recruiter that you are the best candidate for the position and will be an asset to the organization.

Keep in mind that interviewing is not just for the company. It is a two-way street. Be aware of what you see and hear while on company premises to help you decide whether you want to join this particular organization. Don't be too quick to assume anything about any organization. Watch the current employees. Do they appear to enjoy what they're doing, or do you see a lot of long faces? Do you see people standing around drinking coffee at times that are obviously not coffee-break times? Check the workload by looking at the condition of the employees' desks. Notice the bulletin boards around the work areas. Are they covered with memos about rules and regulations, or do you see a mixture of information for the employees about company-planned activities during and after work hours? These are some indicators of the office atmosphere, and they will be helpful to know if and when employment is offered to you. At that point you'll make the important decision about whether to join this organization, and the wrong decision could affect your career while it's still in its early stages.

You may feel uncomfortable with this approach at first, especially if this is your first venture into the full-time job market. After several interviews with different companies, however, you will see distinct differences in the organizational environments. You must select the organization that best reflects your attitude and philosophy about your career. This may sound like a monumental decision, which you may feel unprepared to make, but only you can do it. It really isn't as difficult as it sounds. Your natural feelings will tell you when you're comfortable with your surroundings and the people you deal with. You must consider those feelings immediately after the interview.

The Interview Process

The interview process may vary from company to company but the end product is the same. Some companies require four or five interviews before offering employment, while others may require only one or two. During one of my own job searches, I was asked back for four interviews before being offered a job, and this process took a month and a half. Often the length of the process depends directly on the size of the organization. In some larger companies, one individual is responsible for recruiting in all departments while in smaller companies, the manager of a department is responsible for his or her own recruiting. I have had personal experience with both types of companies, which represent the two extremes of what you can expect in your own job search. Here is a recap of both experiences:

Small company (1,200 employees)	Large company (13,000 employees)
Interview with Personnel Manager	Interview with Personnel Manager
Interview with Department Manager	Interview with Department Manager
Employment offered.	Interview with Operations Manager
	Interview with Facility Manager
	Employment offered.

You must be in tune with the interview process you are involved with. If you are not told about the process for that company, don't be afraid to ask during the first interview. (This process will be covered in greater detail later in this chapter.)

To be successful in the interview process you must be prepared. Try to follow the process from beginning to end. Make notes to yourself about ideas or questions that you feel fit your particular situation. You must be ready for that first interview or more accurately, that first sales meeting.

For the purpose of preparation, we will break the interviewing process down to five steps. Each step will be reviewed in detail so that you can follow it easily while applying your own facts or ideas to the situation. The five steps are as follows:

Step One:	Investigation and Pre-Interview
Step Two:	Opening of the interview
Step Three:	Interview Progression
Step Four:	Closing of the Interview
Step Five:	Recap and Follow-up

Step One

The investigation and pre-interview will help you decide with which companies you would like to have an interview. During this step, try to gather as much information as possible in order to have all the facts you need for a sound decision. You don't need to seek employment with a company that is not sound financially or whose size does not offer you the chance to grow in your area of interest. Before you consider the position itself, the company that is offering the position must pass your inspection.

If you are working with an account representation of a personnel agency, that representative should be your best source of information. Pay careful attention to what the representative tells you about the future of the company and about the future of the position. Most account representatives work on some type of commission, based on number of placements they make within a given period of time. Many representatives will take your career and your job placement seriously, although others strictly regard the placement as a way to increase their commission checks. Remember, this is your career, and the representative should make no decision unless you agree. Don't let him or her send you on interviews with companies unless you are definitely interested in what the company and the position have to offer.

If you are working on your own, check with the public library and the local or state Chamber of Commerce for reports on the company or industry in question, or ask your family and friends what they know about the company. Another good source of information is your local banker. He or she will be helpful in reading and interpreting the financial information printed in the company's annual report. The information you look for should include the following:

—company name and corporate affiliation
—company position within the industry
—products or services offered
—size of organization
—location of facilities
—potential for company growth
—financial position
—company management style
—chances for upward career mobility
—salary growth
—dedication to employees' career development

This information will make you more knowledgeable about the company before your first interview, and will help you decide whether or not you even want to interview with this company.

When I interview applicants, I usually ask, "What do you know about our company?" I am constantly amazed at the number of applicants who respond, "Not very much." Once I was even more amazed when an experienced accountant answered with a mass

38

of information about locations of other facilities, financial data, and projected growth records. None of the information was accurate, however. He had done a lot of research about the wrong company. Make sure you have information about the right company before you start rattling it off in an interview. I can't say which situation would be worse; telling the recruiter you don't know anything about the company or giving all kinds of impressive information about the wrong company.

If you aren't sure about the information you have, call the company and ask the secretary or receptionist for the location of the home office. That office should verify whether you have the correct information. You may ask the receptionist for as much information as she is willing to give, but she may remember who you are and pass that information along to the interviewer. With the basic information that the receptionist can provide, at least you will know which company to research further.

In addition to finding out about the company, make sure you know something about the position you are interviewing for. Again, your account representative will be able to give you the most information. If you responded to an employment ad, you may find the basic information included. If not, the company representative who arranges the interview may be able to give you some information about the duties and responsibilities of the position and where it fits into the organizational structure. Be careful in asking questions of the person who arranged the interview unless that person is knowledgeable about the position. If the department manager asked his or her secretary to call and make the arrangements, chances are the secretary knows very little about the position. Don't put her on the spot by asking a lot of detailed questions that she can't answer. Be assured that she will report your questioning back to the boss in an attempt to justify her inability to answer.

Once you have completed all your homework about the company and the position, you are ready for the actual interview. Your next decision is what to wear. Many books have been written on just this subject, so there is no need to discuss it in detail here. Check with your library for such books. I would simply like to comment that whatever you decide to wear, make sure it is neat, clean, appropriate, and comfortable. It's easy to spot men who are not use to wearing suits and ties as they tug away at their tight collars, and women who are not use to high-heeled shoes as they wobble down the hall.

On the day of the interview, plan your travel so that you arrive no more than five or ten minutes before the designated time. If you arrive earlier, you may give the impression that you're hanging around the office or that you don't have anything else to do. Never arrive at the interview late! The interviewer will consider your tardiness inexcusable and unprofessional, so avoid it unless an emergency arises. If something unavoidable does happen, make sure you call the interviewer as far in advance as possible. Remember, when you call, the interviewer will decide how acceptable your reason is, so it must be good. He or she has that right, which is based on human nature. The interviewer may allow you to come for the interview later that day, or may ask you if you can reschedule for another day, especially if other interviews are scheduled after yours. Here you are at the interviewer's mercy. If you really want the interview and the job, you may have to reschedule other activities to accommodate the interviewer's schedule.

Always carry a small portfolio or briefcase to hold a copy of your resumé, a copy of the PAS you prepared in case you are asked to complete an employment application, and a copy of a national news magazine to help you pass the time in case of unexpected delays in your appointment. Reading will also help you reduce any stress or nervous feelings about the interview. The last thing you want is to appear nervous.

When you arrive, introduce yourself to the secretary or receptionist and state the purpose of your visit. Be pleasant but professional. If you are not sure of the interviewer's name or if it is difficult to pronounce, ask the secretary for the correct pronunciation and spelling. You will need the spelling for the thank-you letter you will send after the interview.

Your interview starts as soon as you walk through the door. The secretary or receptionist will probably make some comment about you to her boss, especially if you do something that she finds amusing or offensive. The secretary's opinion shouldn't matter in the hiring process, but it does with some recruiters.

You may be asked to complete an application, even though you have already submitted a resumé. Always carry a good pen to fill out the application and to take notes during the interview. Don't ask the secretary for a pen: she will think you are unprepared. Your Personal Assessment Sheets should contain most of the information needed to complete the application. I have seen applicants who seemed annoyed by the request to fill out an application, but many companies do this to ensure compliance with their own corporate policies and procedures and to give the nonpersonnel employees a more structured format for reviewing your credentials, so make sure you do a thorough job in completing all information. Leave no question unanswered, if a question doesn't apply, write "N/A" ("Not Applicable") in the space provided. Never write "See resumé" in lieu of a response to the question, even if the secretary says it's okay. She may consider that an acceptable short cut but her boss may have a different opinion and may be the type of individual who is attuned to detail. Your best bet is to be conscientious in completing the application or any other form you are asked to complete.

Once you have filled out the application, you will probably be asked to return it to the secretary. This is another contact with the same person and it gives you another chance to make an impression. Make sure it's a positive one. No doubt she will glance over the application just to find out more about you. Don't worry; this is human nature and anyone would do it. Your credentials will either add to or detract from the original impression you made. Such details as handwriting and the neatness of the application will contribute to this impression. As I said before, this is a buyer-seller relationship, and all these things are part of it. When you're shopping for a new car, don't you look at something more than the make and model?

Shortly after you have finished the application, you can expect to be greeted by your interviewer. This is the beginning of the interview, the second step in the interviewing process.

Step Two

The interview truly begins when you are greeted by the interviewer. The importance of this first greeting cannot be overstated. Make sure you have dressed properly, based on the dress code of that particular company, and that appearance is as good as possible. Your interviewer will form a first impression at the first sight of you. Your appearance, your posture, your manner will add up to this impression, so make it the best you have to offer!

Don't underestimate the factors that make up that first impression. Think about the things you look at when you first meet someone. The facial expression, the neatness of personal grooming, the manner in which their clothes are worn, the handshake offered—all make up that first impression. Don't you form an opinion of that individual as soon as you meet him or her? Of course you do, and so do most people. Pay attention to the personal details that will present the best possible professional image for you. The lack of attention to these details could create a negative first impression, which could prevent you from getting the position you want with this company. Here I would like to give a word of caution, especially to women: everyone in the business world is equal and should respond as an equal. When greeting the interviewer, or anyone else, for that matter, offer a firm handshake without waiting for the other person to offer first.

After the initial greeting, you will probably enter the interviewer's office. If you meet anyone in the hallway on the way to the office, by all means smile and speak, because this may be the next person you see in the interview process.

Once you reach the office, you have entered his or her domain, and all the rules of etiquette should apply. Never smoke during an interview, even if you are offered the opportunity to do so. It is probably a good idea not to smoke before an interview because the smoke tends to linger in your clothes, and a person who doesn't smoke will surely smell it. Nonsmokers are usually highly sensitive to the smell of tobacco smoke.

The interviewer will try to put you at ease by engaging in small talk, which will enable you to become more relaxed and will develop a rapport between the two of you. Not everyone is a born salesman, and some applicants will feel less comfortable than others during the interview process. This is a natural feeling. Even seasoned individuals with a great deal of public exposure are somewhat uncomfortable in an interview, primarily because you must sell yourself during an interview and people are uncomfortable talking about themselves. Just remember to keep yourself under control as well as you can, but don't become too relaxed with all the small talk. You must still act professional.

After the small talk, the interviewer will move on to the purpose of the meeting, and may explain the interview process. If the interviewer mentions other interviewers' names, try to jot them down along with their titles, if titles are mentioned. Make sure you're very attentive during this opening conversation. It could provide you with valuable information that you couldn't obtain during your investigation of the company or the position.

After this stage, the interviewer will go on to the actual interview, which we will discuss in Step Three.

Step Three

During the interview progression, the interviewer will solicit information about you, which will give you the opportunity to sell yourself as the best possible candidate for the position offered by the company. You should realize that the interviewer is at least familiar with the position and has criteria for the candidate that he or she believes would be the best match for this position. During the interview, the recruiter seeks to determine whether you have the necessary qualifications, both personal and professional, to meet these criteria.

Many personnel people who are involved in recruiting take what is often regarded as a negative approach to filling positions. That is, the recruiter assumes automatically that your are not the best candidate for the position. This approach is used for several reasons. First, it forces the recruiter to look at your candidacy objectively. It is an attempt to keep all personal preferences or prejudices out of the selection process. Second, it allows the recruiter to transfer the burden of selecting the candidate back to the candidates themselves. In other words, the candidates must prove themselves and their credentials as the best for the position. This is where the selling part of the job search comes into play. More than in any other part of the job search, you must sell yourself during the interview.

The selling part of the interview can be conducted in a variety of ways. In the primary method, the interviewer asks questions and the candidate must respond. One common rule used by personnel people is the "20-80 rule"—that is, the interviewer talks twenty percent of the time while the applicant talks eighty percent. In this situation the interviewer asks "open-ended" questions, which require the applicant to give more than a simple "yes" or "no" answer. These questions require you to explain or discuss your answers. To help you prepare for this step of the interview, the following pages give a list of sample open-ended questions regarding your personal history, your educational credentials, and your work experience. As you interview with various companies, you can add new questions to your list. This list will help you in future job searches as well as the one in which you are currently involved.

Open-Ended Questions Regarding Personal History

1. How do you define success?

2. What has been your greatest accomplishment thus far?

3. What has been your greatest disappointment thus far?

4. How would you describe yourself to someone you have just met?

5. What are your personal goals for the next five years?

6. What do you feel is your best attribute?

7. What do you feel is your greatest shortcoming?

8. How do you feel this job will fit into your career plans?

9. What are your hobbies or interests.

10. What was the last book that you read?

11. How would you describe your best friend?

12. How do you think your best friend would describe you?

13. Why did you select a career in _____?

14. How does your family feel about this career selection?

15. How did you pay for your education?

16. How do you take criticism?

17. What do people do that irritates you?

18. What was the last movie you saw?

19. What qualifications do you have that make you feel you will be successful?

20. What is your most valued possession?

Open-Ended Questions Regarding Education

1. Why did you select _____ as the place to continue your education?

2. What did you like most about the school?

3. What did you like least about the school?

4. Why did you select _____ as your major area of study?

5. Why did you select_____ as your minor area of study?

6. What was your biggest mistake while attending school?

7. How many hours a week did you use for studying?

8. How has your education prepared you for the job market?

9. What courses did you take that were primarily for enjoyment?

10. What was the topic of your last research paper?

11. How important were your grades to you while in school?

12. What was your grade point average (GPA)?

13. What was your favorite course?

14. What was your least favorite course?

15. What is the best indication of your academic achievement?

16. What school activities were you involved in?

17. Why were you involved in_____ while in school?

18. What did you find as the major difference between high school and college?

19. What courses would you have taken in college had you had the time?

20. What did you like best about college life?

Open-Ended Questions Regarding Work

1. How did you obtain your last job?

2. What do you expect from a company?

3. What can the company expect from you?

4. Why should I hire you?

5. What aspects of your last position did you dislike?

6. What aspects of your last position did you like most?

7. What was a typical day in your last position?

8. What would your last supervisor say about your job performance?

9. How did your past employment prepare you for this job?

10. How would you describe your last company as a place to work?

11. How would you describe your last supervisor?

12. How would you describe the ideal supervisor?

13. Describe your very first job.

14. Why did you leave your last job?

15. What type of position would you like to have in three years?

16. How would you like to have changed your last job?

17. How long do you see yourself in this position?

18. What do you know about our company?

19. Why did you decide to seek a position with this company?

20. How do you define professionalism in the workplace?

In preparing answers for these questions, don't try to memorize a standard answer because some of the questions will be asked in different ways and different circumstances. Not every personnel manager, interviewer, or recruiter uses this list of questions because interviewing is usually based on personal style and preferences. As you prepare, review the answers you plan to give to make sure you have answered the question and provided a logical response. Personnel people are interested not only in what you say but why you say it. Above all, don't give an answer because you think it is what the interviewer wants to hear. If you can't support what you have said or if a later answer contradicts an earlier statement, the interviewer will become confused and won't know which answer to believe. He or she might assume that you are saying what you think someone else wants to hear rather than speaking your feelings. This impression would create a negative feeling about your candidacy.

Practice your answers verbally. Ask a family member or friend to listen to you and offer suggestions if the answer doesn't sound logical. As you practice, keep in mind that while you speak you are also being evaluated on posture, body language, and eye contact. While the interview is taking place, sit straight, but make sure you appear natural and relaxed. Maintain good eye contact with the interviewer; glances away from the interviewer can be interpreted as "deceiving." Always look at the recruiter, but don't offer a cold stare.

Step Four

The closing of the interview will probably be obvious. The interviewer may ask if you have any questions or discuss your availability for future interviews. Sometimes the interviewer will use this time to explain the interview process of the company. In any case, don't linger when you know the interviewer is trying to close.

Now is a good time to recap one or two of your leading qualifications and how they would apply to the duties and responsibilities of the position you want. Beyond that, don't give the impression that you are desperate for the position and that you are twisting the recruiter's arm to hire you. A word of caution is in order here. Being assured about your qualifications may be regarded as arrogant by some personnel people, but others may consider it a desirable sign of aggressiveness.

During the interview you have had a chance to learn something about the interviewer and to read his or her style. With this information you should know best how to close the interview. If you are naturally unaggressive, don't try to be aggressive during the closing; it will appear unnatural.

After you have closed, always express your appreciation for the interview and show enthusiasm for another interview, if that is a part of the interview process. If the interview process has not been discussed, ask about the next step in a way that doesn't require you to make assumptions about the success of the first one. Ask questions such as, "If I am considered further, what is the next step in the interview process?" This question doesn't require immediate feedback from the interviewer. You simply want to know what to expect. A professional personnel manager or recruiter should volunteer that information.

Step Five

Immediately after the interview or after you have left the company premises, take some time to review the interview in depth. Make a list of the questions that the interviewer asked during the interview, with some comments on the answers you gave. You may hear some of those questions again in future interviews with that company if you are called back to continue the process. Try to make an honest personal evaluation of your performance in the interview. If you think you had some rough spots, make notes of them so that you can brush up before the next interview.

The next part of the recap and follow-up is to make a list of the duties and responsibilities of the position as they were presented to you during the first interview. This will be helpful if you are interviewing with several companies at the same time. You may mix up the various positions and companies especially if there is a long time between interviews.

Record as much as possible about the company, the interviewer, and the position, and make any other notes that may be valuable during a second interview. If you are involved in a lengthy interview process that takes place over three or four weeks, it will be difficult to remember everything without writing it down.

You may wish to use the sample form which follows to recap your interview. Keep your recaps on file until you have landed the position you are looking for. If you are unsuccessful in this attempt but want to work at this company, you may want to hold on to these notes until you have another opportunity to interview with some of these people. These notes have many uses; the minute you toss them in the trash, you will probably discover another use.

Company_____

Interviewer_____ Title_____

Position interviewed for_____

Duties and responsibilities_____

_____

_____

Qualifications for position_____

_____

Next interview (time/date)_____ Next interviewer_____

_____

Within a short time, send a short note to the interviewer. This note serves two purposes: it serves as an honest thank-you to the interviewer for the time and consideration that he or she has shown, and it serves to remind the interviewer who you are and what some of your qualifications for the position are. I have received many formal cards from applicants to thank me for the interview, and although I thought it was a nice gesture, I couldn't help wondering why they didn't send a professional note trying to sell themselves. In the business world, I personally don't think a social thank-you card is appropriate.

It is important that your letter arrive at the proper time. If the first phase of interviewing took place at the beginning of the week and you were among the first to be interviewed, your letter should arrive near the end of the week. If you were interviewed at the end of the week, your thank-you letter should arrive immediately. You need that contact with the interviewer when the second round of the interviews is being considered.

Personnel people have different views about phoning as a means of following up an interview. Some of them feel that a person involved in interviewing doesn't want to be bothered by a telephone call. You are probably the best one to make that decision, based on what you know about the interviewer. It is not necessary to call, but if you decide to make that call, be precise and to the point. You may ask about the status of the position for which you applied and thank the interviewer for the interview. If you call and if you also sent a thank-you letter, make sure that at least a week has passed since the interviewer received your letter. A letter and a phone call in a very short period of time are too much. Timing is the most important part of each method of follow-up.

In the following pages you will find two sample thank-you letters that can be used as examples. Try to incorporate the specifics of your interview into this type of letter. The samples are precise, and represent standard business practices.

As for the paper and ink to use in writing thank-you letters, follow the same guidelines as in the presentation of your resumé. It would be best to use the same paper and print that you used in your resumé. This would serve as a subtle reminder of who you are. Believe me, after many interviews, the candidates all start to blend together. The interviewer *needs* reminding.

Tips for Subsequent Interviews

1. Treat all subsequent interviews in the same professional manner as you did the first. Never try to enter an interview without being prepared. Review any rough spots you noted in the first interview.

2. Don't be sure of getting the job until it has been offered to you. Applicants often interpret what one interviewer says as assurance that they will be offered the position. Keep in mind that one interviewer may not have the final say.

3. Never discuss salary during the first interview. Wait for the interviewer to bring up the subject during all later interviews.

4. When discussing money, be noncommital about exact amounts until you are sure you are a serious candidate for the position. If you are called back for a second or third interview, you can assume that you are a serious candidate. If you are asked to name an exact amount, state that you have some excellent qualifications to offer, but you realize that you have limited experience

and will need to prove yourself to the organization. At that point, you may want to state a minimum salary that will be acceptable.

There is nothing wrong with asking what salary range has been set for the position. If you are working with an account representative, he or she should have told you what salary the position carries. If this is the case, the conversation about salary might be a short one. Whatever the salary is, make sure it fits your financial needs. Accepting less could create problems for you before your career gets started.

5. Complete an interview recap after each interview. Make notes of any unusual questions and use them to prepare for later interviews.

6. Send a thank-you letter to each interviewer. Be sure that each letter is somewhat different from the others, because letters like this are often passed around to everyone in the interview process. Add a personal touch for each interviewer. No one wants to see form letters addressed to different people. Then, if the letters are passed around, they can only enhance your position as an applicant.

Whatever you do, don't stop your job search after an interview with one company. Keep the interview process going until you have reported to work at a job you want, at a company that offers you a chance for career development. Settling for a less desirable position just for the sake of having a job could, and probably would, complicate your career path. Most important, your search is not a success unless you have the job you wanted. After all, your career should be more than a job. It should be enjoyable.

Sample Thank-You Letter

1814 Victoria Lane
Montgomery, Alabama 36193
October, 1984

Mr. Robert Guest
Director of Personnel
Cambridge Manufacturing Company
Montgomery, Alabama 36193

Dear Mr. Guest:

Thank you for the opportunity to talk with you about the position of manager trainee in your Phenix City facility. Your company's total commitment to its employees is obvious by the friendly atmosphere demonstrated by the employees as they go about their daily routine. I would like very much to be a part of the Cambridge organization for that reason.

I believe my degree in Business Administration, along with my keen desire to learn, would be a tremendous asset to Cambridge as they begin the next manager trainee group. This commitment to training is unmatched by any other company that I am familiar with and would allow me to learn first hand about the art of management.

I would appreciate the opportunity to further discuss my credentials and career goals with other members of your management team and look forward to hearing from you again in the near future.

Sincerely yours,

Randall Myers

Sample Thank-You Letter

1401 Village Lane
Harrisonburg, VA 22801
May 5, 1985

Mr. George Manard
Foxmore Publishing Company
860 North Industrial Blvd.
Greensboro, North Carolina 2742

Dear Mr. Manard:

I appreciate your taking the time to talk with me yesterday about the trainee position in your Marketing Department. Your facilities are very impressive, and your staff was extremely kind during my visit.

Our talk solidified my belief that my educational experience along with my ability to be creative would be an asset to your company. With this foundation and your comapny's committment to training, I would be able to grow and learn from you and your existing staff.

Thanks again for your time and consideration. Please let me know if I can provide any additional information for you.

Sincerely,

Mary Brevard

A "Do" List For The Interview

1. Arrive five to ten minutes before the designated time.

2. Remember, you are a guest of the company and should be pleasant to everyone regardless of their position.

3. Always sit straight and be alert.

4. Fill out all forms and application completely, accurately and neatly.

5. Dress appropriately in neat, professional attire.

6. Wait to be invited before sitting.

7. Offer a firm handshake regardless of sex.

8. Maintain eye contact with interviewer.

9. Do not criticize former employers or others.

10. Refrain from smoking or chewing gum.

11. When answering the interviewer's questions, be positive and direct.

12. Thank the interviewer for his or her time.

13. Write a follow-up letter to the interviewer.

CHAPTER SEVEN

The Questions Most Often Asked

* **About The Job Search**

* **About The Resumé**

* **About The Interview**

* About The Job Search

How should I dress for the interview?

Your choice of clothing is an important part of the interview. Personnel managers, interviewers, and recruiters are all human, and they allow the first impression to play a significant role in their recruiting process. Remember, the interviewer must evaluate you not only for your skills and ability to do the job, but also for your ability to mesh with the existing work force. If you appear for the interview either in high-fashion clothes or in styles not acceptable in the business world, you may create negative reactions. Overdressing is as detrimental as underdressing. If you are working with an agency, the representative should be able to tell you exactly how to dress for that particular company. Companies can vary greatly in their dress codes, so ask about each company. If you are conducting your own job search, drive past the company as employees are leaving at the end of the day and make your own evaluation of what dress would be appropriate. Whatever you choose to wear, make sure it is clean and freshly pressed.

If you are traveling out of town for the interview, take several different styles of clothes to wear. You may be able to do some quick evaluating when you arrive. Knowing the dress code before you go for the interview could save you some embarrassment and allow you to blend into the company atmosphere.

Is it acceptable to take notes during the interview?

As a personnel manager, I have no objections to an applicant taking notes. In fact, I think it is becoming common practice in the job search process, especially because the search is now viewed in a more structured manner. If you want to take notes, ask the interviewer whether he or she objects. In any case, don't let your note-taking distract the interviewer and don't let it monopolize your time or attention. It should not be obvious that you are taking notes.

What is the interview process in most companies?

It is hard to describe the process in exact terms because it varies so much from company to company. The process used in each company is influenced by many factors including the size of the organization, the company's approach to recruiting, and even the type of position offered. Generally speaking, the smaller companies work with a single or bilevel process, while larger companies work with a multilevel process. This process might consist of an interview with the personnel manager and then the department head and maybe a division head, depending on the organizational structure.

Remember that every person you must talk with in the process of getting a job has a different personality and that makes your task more difficult. This is why recapping each interview is so important. Not only are you recapping the company and the position; you are also recapping each individual recruiter.

Is it unusual to ask about the organizational structure during the interview?

No, not at all. Remember, you are looking for a position that will offer you visibility and a chance to grow, and the structure of an organization may be a deciding factor in your job selection. There is nothing wrong with asking, "Where does this position fit into the department's organizational structure?" If the position isn't clear to you, you could ask, "What is the logical career path from this position?" Listen carefully to the answers. If the interviewer isn't clear about the career path, this could indicate that this company doesn't concern itself with career paths or development. This area should be important to you. After all, it is your career.

How much detail should I give in an answer to a question during the interview?

When asked a question in the interview, the only thing that's necessary is to answer the question. You must remember this point to be successful in the interviewing process. Don't tell the interviewer everything you know about the subject. The interviewer expects you to do most of the talking (remember the 20-80 Rule), but don't be so long-winded that the interviewer has to interrupt you to ask a question. Keep the interview on a comfortable level and regard it as a natural conversation with the interviewer. Be comfortable and professional, and your answers will flow accordingly. Any attempt to impress the interviewer with a vast amount of knowledge will surely be interpreted as an attempt to impress the company. If you know what you're looking for in your career and if you know your credentials, you're prepared. Be natural and everything will go well.

If I don't get the position, should I ask the interviewer the reason?

Some interviewers will give you an honest answer but the majority will give you a legally acceptable response, such as, "We offered the position to someone we felt had a stronger technical background," or "We hired someone with a master's degree in business." Because of the legalities involved in personnel work, most recruiters are not willing to give you an honest answer and generally suspect anyone who asks. Depending on the rapport you have built with the interviewer, however, you might get an honest response.

If you decide to ask, don't try to defend yourself if you get an unfavorable response. The decision has been made about this position and there is nothing you can do but that doesn't close the door on your chances for future positions. Don't resort to unprofessional behavior if you didn't get the job, but simply ask whether you might be considered for future positions if any develop. Your actions in handling this disappointment could be a positive influence on your candidacy in the future. No one wants to hire a poor loser.

If you are fortunate enough to receive an honest answer, take it as constructive criticism but don't change your entire personality or your view of your career plans. This is only one company; the experience and the information you receive will be helpful, but it is not the last word.

If I have ever been fired from a job, should I discuss this during the interview?

Yes, by all means. Failure to do so could cause people, especially the interviewer, to think you have something to hide. If, in fact, you have been fired, discussing it at the appropriate time, will alert the employer. You can be sure that when reference checks are made on you, some aspect of the termination will come up. It may be even your former employer's refusal to offer any comments about your employment except to say that you were employed for a stated period of time. The fact that you have brought up the subject puts you in a more favorable light, and it also allows you to tell the interviewer your side of the story. On the other hand, if he or she learns of the termination from your previous employer, it could surprise him, and he may wonder why you didn't discuss it during the interview.

When a person is fired, he or she always tends to blame the employer and not to shoulder any of the blame. When discussing the circumstances of your termination, don't express any negative feelings about the previous employer, even if you feel that he or she was completely wrong in their actions. Let the interviewer be the judge. Be sure you explain what happened and why you feel that it should or shouldn't have resulted in your termination. Above all, be completely honest and don't slant your side of the incident in the least.

One of my applicants discussed one of his terminations, his third in a five-year work career. He gave me a detailed account of every incident leading to his termination, and as he completed the details of his latest firing, he stated, "Sir, I wouldn't blame you if you didn't offer me a position with your company because it appears that I am not willing to adjust to a company's rules, but I think I can. After losing three jobs, I am convinced that my way of thinking in the past has been wrong. I only want a chance to prove that." I offered him a position.

Should I ask about performance appraisals and salary reviews during the interview?

Yes and no. You can bring up the subject of performance appraisals during the first interview when you talk about career development and career paths, but you shouldn't bring in salary reviews in the first interview. That should be left to a later interview, preferably if the interviewer mentions it first. If you let the interviewer mention salary review first, you may gain valuable information about what salary the company will offer you if you are among the candidates for the job. If you have done your homework, you know what your salary requirements are.

* About The Resumé

Is there any advantage to using a resumé rather than filling out the company's employment application?

Yes, there is an advantage to using the resumé. In your resumé, you have complete control over all the information. You alone decide what will and will not be included and in what format the information will be presented. With this type of control, you can present yourself on paper in the most favorable light. In using the employment application as your only source of information, you are forced to present yourself according to someone else's criteria. It may not allow you to include some of the information you would like to give.

It is not unusual to be asked to complete an application after you have been contacted for an interview. If this happens, you may want to turn in a resumé along with the completed application. If the interviewer already has a copy of your resumé, the duplication won't hurt.

Should I pay someone to write my resumé?

You could do this, but I don't advise it for several reasons. Most importantly, you know yourself better than anyone else, and you would have to go over all the information with the person you selected to write your resumé. Something could get lost in the process. You need to know everything that is included so that you can explain it. Secondly, the process we have discussed in this book has prepared you for the final step, the interview. By constructing a PAS, you have reviewed facts and information that might come up during the interview. Being prepared is the best way to deal with the jitters that are so common when people go for interviews. Although the resumé is very important, the interview is even more important. If you choose to have someone write your resumé for you, you will not be as well prepared as if you had written the resumé yourself.

Is a career objective necessary on my resumé?

On a scale of one to ten, I would say that the need for a career objective on your resumé ranks somewhere between a six and a ten. I know this sounds strange, but it depends on the size of the company as well as the type of position. Smaller companies are less interested in career objective because their organizations don't have a lot of room for upward mobility. If the company is a larger one, the career objective is more important.

Should I list individual courses that I took in school?

This isn't necessary unless you are involved in a highly technical area, such as data processing. You may want to include a brief listing of your "specialty" course, such as the name of the computer language you studied. I would say that this is the only exception to the guideline. Remember, the recruiter should be aware of the courses involved in the degrees that the company is looking for during the employee search, so listing the regular courses should not be necessary. If you take the time to make a list of all your courses, or better yet, obtain a copy of your transcript, it might come in handy. The application for employment is sometimes very detailed, and it might ask about some of your courses.

Should I attach letters of recommendation to my resumé?

This isn't necessary, and the letters probably wouldn't be read if you did enclose them. You have stated on your resumé that references are available on request. Take copies of the letters of recommendation to the interview, so that you can present them if you are asked for them. Be sure you have plenty of copies when you go for the interview; don't ask the interviewer to make copies for you.

Should I attach reference information obtained through the university placement office?

It isn't necessary, but it won't hurt. Again, I suggest you base the decision on the type of company you are interviewing with. Companies that work directly with certain universities have established procedures that incorporate the use of standardized forms for this purpose. In cases like this, the company may ask the college placement office to provide them with certain information on each applicant and the school will change their forms to comply with the request. Normally, if the company wants information from the college, they may ask you to submit the information or to sign a company form that allows the information to be sent directly to the company.

What type of special achievements should I list on my resumé?

List any achievement that required an effort on your part and was not strictly a popularity contest. Achievement such as the dean's list, honor societies, professional fraternities and sororities, and faculty awards show that you had to do something to earn them. Don't forget to include any outstanding achievements from your high school years, including scouting, church, and civic activities.

* About The Job Search

Should I rely on a personnel agency to conduct my job search?

Working with a representative from a personnel agency can be a great benefit during your job search. He or she can assist you in finding out more about available positions and about the companies that offer those positions. A representative can also help you gain more inside information about organizational philosophy, structure, and growth projection. Another advantage to working with an agency is that the representatives know the job market and work directly with the interviewing company on your behalf.

If you decide to work with an agency, try to find one that makes placement exclusively in your career field. Such an agency will be better informed about the field in general and better able to answer your questions about salaries in the field, expected benefits, and career paths. Don't be afraid to ask questions; it's your career. Often the representative becomes so involved in day-to-day work that he assumes you understand certain aspects of the job search, while you have no idea what's going on. You must be the one who controls the search. If you don't understand something, say so and ask for an explanation. Don't let the representative place you in a position unless you are 100 percent sold on it.

Should I pay an agency fee?

This is a very common question these days. I wouldn't consider paying a fee for a position because doing so would be almost like saying that my credentials weren't good enough to qualify on their own. Paying an agency fee is like paying your own salary for a while so that you can prove your worth to the company. If the company wants to recruit people with the skills they need, they should be willing to pay the personnel agency's fee.

Should I use newspaper employment ads in my job search?

In conducting a job search you should use every available source of information. The general rule is that 20 percent of the available positions can be found in the employment advertisements in the newspaper. Use them with this in mind, but don't make them the only source of employment information. Use ads to collect information about the various positions available, qualifications, benefits, and the salaries currently being paid for similar positions. This information can be used as a basis of comparison for other positions you are seeking.

The Sunday editions of the larger city newspapers usually carry the greatest number of employment ads. Review the newspaper constantly, and pursue any and all positions that your qualifications meet. People have discovered excellent positions while casually reading the paper, when they spotted a job that interested them even though they weren't looking to change positions.

Whom should I use as references?

Your references should be people who know you and who can give your prospective employer an accurate picture in light of their knowledge of you. Not all references will know you in the same way. Logically, you will want to list only those individuals who you know will give you a good professional reference. Know each individual well before you name him or her as a reference.

Do employers really check references?

Because of the legal issues that are constantly raised in the area of employment, I would venture to guess that at least 85 percent of all references are checked in one way or another. Your prospective employer may know someone who works at your former employer's business or may have a friend who can check your references with someone he knows. This may not be totally legal, but it happens. This type of reference checking is very common in small towns. More formal reference checking is sometimes done over the phone, and many references are checked in writing to satisfy some legal or corporate requirements.

Should I send a copy of my school transcript to prospective employers?

This is not advisable unless the employer asks for it. Keep in mind that the recruiter or personnel manager receives a tremendous amount of mail, especially if an advertisement has been placed in the newspaper. By dumping more paper on the recruiter, you are not helping the situation. Your resumé should be prepared in such a way that it will invite more contact and perhaps a request for additional information, which might include a request for your transcript.

Should I send out unsolicited resumés?

Absolutely, especially to companies at which you would like to work and for which you feel you have the qualifications. Because only 20 percent of all jobs are listed in the newspaper, you may not see any positions advertised, but openings that are never advertised do exist. I have spoken with many personnel people who feel advertising, especially in a mass medium such as the newspaper, is the last resort in the field of recruiting for some positions. The normal flow of applications and resumés sometimes makes advertising unnecessary, so positions that open up in these companies never seem to reach the public eye. For this reason, send unsolicited resumés by all means. Remember, though, that your chance of a response is slim unless the company is interested in pursuing your candidacy further. It is proper to make a phone call to the company several days after you know they have received your resumé, and a call will give the personnel people a chance to hear your name. If you make such a call, it's important to comment briefly about your qualifications and to say why you want to work for that particular company. Beyond that contact, you should not call the company again unless you know of a specific position that is available.

What about employment contracts?

Employment contracts are normally found among top executives, but are also occasionally at other levels of management in certain industries. The textile and apparel industry and some sales positions use employment contracts.

Since you are relatively new to a career-type position, I would not advise you to sign any type of employment contract. Although there are definite advantages to being under contract, there are also disadvantages. Some employment contracts have clauses that restrict your geographical areas of employment if you should decide to leave the organization before the end of the contract period. Before you sign, the employment contract should be reviewed by an attorney with experience in this area of the law. Don't be so zealous about getting a job that you toss logic out the window.

How long does the average job search last?

Many college seniors ask this question because they don't know when they should start seeking postgraduate employment. Depending on the field you have chosen for your career, the job search could last anywhere from a week to six months. Some people never find the particular position for which their education prepared them. In those cases, they took a first job to hold them until they could locate and land the job of their dreams. I'm sure you've heard stories of someone who was hired after only one interview session, but in other cases the job search has taken as long as six months. I wish I could tell you that a job search can be completed within a specific time, but I would be foolish to say so, and you would be foolish if you believed me.

The outcome of the job search depends largely on you. You can continue your job search long after you graduate if you have been unable to find the job you are looking for. Don't be discouraged if this happens. Believe me, others have survived it.